The Business of Me

Your Job … Your Career … Your Value

By:

Linwood Bailey

iUniverse, Inc.
Bloomington

The Business of Me
Your Job ... Your Career ... Your Value

iUniverse books may be ordered through booksellers or by contacting:

iUniverse
1663 Liberty Drive
Bloomington, IN 47403
www.iuniverse.com
1-800-Authors (1-800-288-4677)

ISBN: 978-1-4697-7382-7 (sc)
ISBN: 978-1-4697-7383-4 (hc)
ISBN: 978-1-4697-7384-1 (e)

Library of Congress Control Number: 2012903048

Printed in the United States of America

iUniverse rev. date: 4/6/2012

Linwood Bailey
52070 Sherford Court
Granger, IN 46530
linwood@fieldsofsuccesscoaching.com
www.fieldsofsuccesscoaching.com

To today's business professionals, who keep the business of America running despite the career management and employment challenges they face.

In memory of my grandparents, Robert and Lillie Ballard, who provided education for life and shaped possibilities for my future.

For my mother, Christine Bailey, who taught me to view the challenges of life as opportunities to achieve.

"Information is a source of learning. But unless it is organized, processed, and available to the right people in a format for decision making, it is a burden, not a benefit."

—C. William Pollard, former CEO of ServiceMaster and author of the best-selling book *The Soul of the Firm*

Note from Author

Thank you for picking up this book or continuing your Internet search for information to address your career management and employment concerns. *The Business of Me: Your Job … Your Career … Your Value* provides steps, tools, resources, and information to help you maintain employment, find a job, get pay raises, and get promoted to maintain or even increase your standard of living.

The Business of Me recognizes that there is an abundance of career management data available from other books, the Internet, and the media. The uniqueness of *The Business of Me* is in its design—a structure that will enable you to evaluate and manage the abundance of data available to you. Using it will help you move forward in your job, your career, and your life.

Contents

Acknowledgments

The Business of Me is the product of my life experiences, research, and the advice, wisdom, and support of many people. Following is a partial list of numerous people to whom I owe my deepest gratitude.

JoAnn, whose encouragement and support has sustained me, not only while writing this book, but also throughout forty years of being my wife, companion, and most trusted confidante.

My close friend, Ed Benedict, who introduced me to the coaching profession, encouraged me to write this book, helped me communicate my ideas, and is always there no matter the difficulty of the situation.

Darryl Poole, whose very positive feedback on my newsletters and whose persistence encouraged me to write this book.

Virginia Hayden, my first boss in industry, from whom I learned the importance of personal development and caring for the people I managed.

My friend and former boss, Fay Billings, who challenged me to think beyond my comfort zone.

My sister, Jean Braxton, who has made her concern for my well-being a lifelong, 24/7 endeavor with no strings attached.

My sister, Sandra Bailey, who encouraged me to look beyond what I could do well to how I could make a difference in the lives of others.

Donna Smith-Bellinger, my personal coach, for the suggestions on presenting several concepts included in this book.

Introduction

The March 23, 2009 "Annual Special Issue" of *Time* Magazine presented "10 Ideas Changing the World Right Now." The first idea presented was "Why Your Job Is Your Most Valuable Asset." The article discussed the importance individuals had placed on the value of their homes and investment portfolios and how these assets lost significant value during the recent economic downturn. As the dust settled from the downturn, people have begun to reflect on how they accumulated their real estate holdings and other investments. People have rediscovered that source—their jobs.

Our jobs and our careers provide the path to fulfilling our hopes and dreams—the best that life can offer. This includes the homes we want to own, the cars we want to drive, the education we want for our children, and the financial security we want to achieve during our working and retirement years. Managing your most important economic assets—your job and career—will enable you to get promotions and pay raises, land new career opportunities, and maintain your employment to provide the value you need to accumulate to fulfill your hopes and dreams.

Yet, professionals working in today's business world are finding that getting value from their careers has become quite a challenge due to the unprecedented business challenges that companies are encountering. These business challenges include global competition, rapid changes in the marketplace, shorter product life cycles, constant pressure on profit margins, and meeting the quarterly expectations of the investment community. Companies have taken various measures to respond to these challenges, including downsizing, restructuring, implementing new business models, and changing the way that individual employees are utilized and evaluated. As a consequence, today's professionals are faced with fewer opportunities for promotion, intense competition for the fewer opportunities, increased difficulty getting pay raises to maintain their standard of living, and higher risks of experiencing interruptions in their employment. And finding a job after losing one has become much more challenging.

The career challenges that today's professionals encounter have not gone unnoticed. There is an abundance of career management data available from numerous sources. Career counselors, coaches, and others involved in providing career advice provide tidbits of data during appearances on CNN, MSNBC, CNBC, and television talk shows. Yahoo, Google, and other sites on the Internet frequently provide career advice. Career advice books are abundant at Barnes & Noble, Amazon, and other brick and mortar and Internet-based bookstores. It is easy to feel overloaded, bombarded, and even confused by all the data coming from so many sources. The data is not structured in a way that makes it easy to address your career goals and objectives or the specific career situations you are facing.

Without a structure, you can find yourself *going in circles*—doing a lot, but achieving very little. You may be stuck in a job that offers no potential for personal growth, struggling to keep up with increases in the cost of living, worried that you may be a victim of your company's next downsizing, or watching the months pass without being employed.

Given the challenges you face and the enormous amount of data coming at you, what can you do to get the most value from your most important economic asset—your career?

There is a proven structure for creating value from assets. It is rooted in business management. After all, companies exist to create value for their stakeholders. The structure that companies use is the proven and age-old Business Management Process.

The Business of Me: Your Job ... Your Career ... Your Value explains how you can apply the Business Management Process to manage your career. The business management principles, processes, and career management information and tools in *The Business of Me* are supplemented by real-life examples, and the thirty-four years of the author's experience. Linwood Bailey managed people and functions in multiple industries and corporate cultures. He experienced what today's professionals are experiencing, being the decision maker that impacted careers, as well as being impacted by decisions made by the companies for which he worked.

Business Management and *The Business of Me*

The Business Management Process includes execution of the following steps:

1. Build a value foundation
    a. Develop the product
    b. Brand the product
2. Market
3. Sell
4. Deliver
5. Learn and adjust

Companies build their value creation foundation by developing products that satisfy the needs of their customers.

Companies build on their value creation foundation by establishing brands. By establishing brands, companies communicate a reason to buy their products and distinguish their products from those offered by their competitors.

Companies market their brands by identifying who may buy their brands and then making potential buyers aware of the benefits they will realize if they purchase the brands.

Through selling, companies convince people to buy their brands. They convert potential buyers into customers.

Once people are convinced to purchase, companies deliver on their brand promises to ensure that customers will reward them with repeated purchases.

Companies learn and adjust to ensure that they continue to create value. Learning and adjusting is based on information companies receive during the development, branding, marketing, selling, and delivery of their products.

The Business of Me: Your Job ... Your Career ... Your Value will explain how you can apply the Business Management Process to managing your most important economic asset—your career.

Business Management Process	*The Business of Me* Application
Develop the product	Turn skills and capabilities into something you can offer for value
Brand the product	Define and express the value you offer
Market	Get known for what you offer
Sell	Convince decision makers to hire or promote you
Deliver	Prove your value by managing your job performance
Learn and adjust	Maintain and even increase the value of your skills and capabilities

The Business of Me provides a structure as well as a "virtual filing cabinet" for managing your career to create value.

- Structure for determining:
  - What steps do you need to take?
  - How can you optimize the use of your time, money, and other resources?
  - What resources and tools can you use, and when should you use them?
- Virtual filing cabinet
  - What information do you need?
  - How can you use the information?
  - When should you use the information?

Guide for Reading *The Business of Me*

The Business of Me presents the application of the Business Management Process to the management of your career in four sections:

1. Build Your Value Foundation
     Develop Your Product: Define What You Offer
     Brand Your Product: Make Yourself Unique
2. Get Your Value in Gear
     Market: Let Them Know What You Can Offer
     Sell: Get Hired
3. Prove Your Value
     Deliver: Provide What You Promise
4. Maintain/Increase Your Value
     Learn & Adjust: Keep Up with Change

Each chapter in *The Business of Me* starts with a quote and a question that conveys the core concept of the chapter. This is followed by a synopsis of the component of the Business Management Process that is the focus of the chapter.

Synopses of Business Management Process components are followed by applications of the components to career management—*The Business of Me* Process.

Chapters end with a summary that recaps the structure covered in the chapter—the specific steps for executing the component of *The Business of Me* Process. Chapter summaries also include a filing cabinet that relates information provided in the chapters to specific career management situations and needs.

As you read *The Business of Me*, you will notice the interdependency among components of the process. This provides continuity from component to component and facilitates the use of *The Business of*

Me as your point of reference for evaluating the abundance of career management information that is available to you beyond this book.

As a strong believer in the Learn and Adjust component of *The Business of Me*, I invite you to provide your feedback and comments on your reading experience by visiting www.BusinessOfMeBook.com.

Section I

Build Your Value Foundation
- Develop Your Product: Define What You Offer
- Brand Your Product: Make Yourself Unique

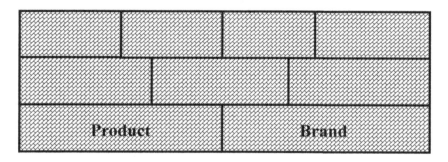

Build Your Value Foundation

Successful companies recognize that value creation starts with offering products that satisfy the needs of their potential customers—their target market. Recognizing that there are other companies that also offer products that could satisfy the needs of their target market, companies brand their products so that their products stand out versus the products offered by their competitors.

Chapters one and two explain how you can apply the Business Management Process to develop and brand your personal product to establish a foundation for creating personal value. The chapters will explain how to convert your strengths, capabilities, and skills into your personal product and how to make your product (you) stand out versus your competitors for promotions, raises, positions, and new career opportunities.

Chapter 1:

Develop Your Product: Define What You Offer

"Business is not just doing deals; business is having great products."
—Ross Perot

What do I offer—why would anyone hire or promote me?

Product Development: Business Management Process

The core measure of business success is value creation. At the heart of value creation is the offering of products that satisfy the customer's needs. This sounds so fundamental and simple, yet companies from large to sole proprietors can sometimes lose sight of this critical factor. In *Positioning: The Battle for Your Mind,* Al Ries and Jack Trout cited failures that companies experienced when they touted their expertise in financial management and other competencies as predictors of success as they introduced new products. After the products failed in the marketplace, the companies realized that the products were not successful because they did not satisfy the needs of customers more than products offered by their competitors. The companies realized that operational excellence is *important,* but developing and offering products that satisfy the needs of the customer is *critical*.

The Product Development component of the Business Management Process includes five basic steps:

1. Assess company's strengths and capabilities.
2. Research the marketplace to identify opportunities based on the company's capabilities and strengths.
3. Develop a product concept.
4. Develop a prototype.
5. Develop the product to be introduced into the marketplace.

Executing steps 1 and 2 focuses the Product Development Process on what products the company should develop.

Step 3 defines the features the product must offer to satisfy the market needs identified in Step 2 and provides the basis for the development of prototypes.

Prototypes serve as models of what the final product must offer and provide the foundation for establishing the product development plan.

The execution of the product development plan closes the gap between what is required to satisfy the needs of the market and what the company already has in order to achieve that goal. Closing the gap could include actions such as acquiring equipment and technical expertise, redesigning or creating new business processes, and training employees.

Product Development: *The Business of Me*

Companies organize functions such as finance, information technology, engineering, marketing, and sales to support business operations and the execution of business strategies. In performing your job responsibilities as a member of a business function, you can easily overlook that you are providing a product to satisfy the needs of a customer. That product is your skills and capabilities. The customer is your function, boss, and other functions and individuals who depend on you to perform their responsibilities. The value you create for yourself is your compensation—your base salary, bonus, and benefits. By reading this chapter, you will:

1. Gain an understanding of the essential role that Personal Product Development serves in managing your career.
2. Be introduced to a process that you can use to convert your skills and capabilities into a personal product that will create value for you.
3. Be alerted to resources and tools that you can use to enable the development of your personal product.

Let's apply the Product Development component of the Business Management Process to the development of your personal product.

Assess Your Strengths, Capabilities, and Skills

There are several assessments designed to help you identify your strengths. Assessments establish profiles of you based on the answers you provide to questions related to your interests, likes and dislikes, and how you act in certain situations. These profiles provide themes or terms that describe situations, roles, or assignments in which you will be most effective. Your profiles are ranked in order of your most to least dominant strengths.

Assessments are also available to help you identify your strongest capabilities and skills. As with the assessments designed to help you identify your strengths, skills assessments rank your skills in the order of your level of proficiency. Skills assessments focus on:

- Measuring your natural abilities.
- Defining your interests.
- Inventorying your skills.
- Relating your personality and psychological type(s) to occupations and job roles.

Some assessments are available on the Internet, either for a fee or gratis. Many career counselors, human resources professionals, and coaches are qualified to administer assessments. Your company may provide assessments at no cost to you.

Also, do not overlook the valuable input that you can receive from people who know you well—your peers, supervisors, friends, and even family members. My own interest in coaching was sparked by a close friend, Ed, who listened to a friend describe coaching—how it included relating to people, being able to listen and provide feedback, and making a difference in the lives of people. Ed recalled his observations of me during our friendship of over twenty years and how coaching reflected how I related to people and the impact that I had on them.

Ed said, "Why don't you take a look at coaching as your next career after you retire from the corporate world?"

Ed gave his friend's phone number to me. When I called her, she provided more information on coaching, identified a book on coaching to familiarize me with the coaching profession, and identified a program that could train me to be a coach.

My interest was further supported by my sister, Sandra. When I expressed my intention to become a coach, she said, "I'm surprised that you didn't pursue this earlier in your life." She spoke of how I had coached family members and friends through challenging situations and also told me of her son's admiration for how I relate to people. In his middle school poem about his favorite relatives, Adrian said, "My uncle has never met a stranger."

You can gain insight into your strengths and skills by conducting an exercise I observed in a class of MBA candidates in a leadership course at Indiana University-South Bend. The premise of the exercise is that we perform at our best when we focus our strengths on what we encounter or are assigned to do. The exercise requires students to:

1. List three to five of their most significant accomplishments.
2. List three to five things that they did not perform well.
3. Ask individuals who have worked with them, observed them, or know them to list three to five things that they performed well and three to five things that they did not perform well.

Students pinpoint their strengths by asking, "What strengths are reflected across my accomplishments?" Students compare their answers to this question to the answers provided by the individuals they asked to participate in the exercise.

By identifying their strengths, students are able to focus their job searches and/or pursue opportunities that present the best chances for their success.

Research the Marketplace

With the assessment you've done, you've discovered quite a bit about yourself. You have a good understanding of your strengths and skills. Now, how can you target the development of your skills and capabilities? How can you focus your personal product development efforts? How can you set a framework to guide your efforts? How can you make the best use of your resources and time?

I recommend that you establish a **Target Position Description** to answer these questions. Following are the steps for developing your Target Position Description:

1. Set a period of time for developing your product.
2. Focus on a position to which you will aspire. This is your target position.
3. Conduct research and gather information on what the employment market requires for your target position.
4. Prepare a description of your target position.

There are two approaches to setting the period of time for developing your product. You can take a long-term view—perhaps five years into the future—or choose a shorter period of time. Either approach can be successful; it's a matter of personal preference and focus. Some people prefer the long-term view because it enables them to view short-term trends and developments within the context of their career goals and helps them when they need to make career trade-offs and decisions.

Others prefer the short-term view because they are not certain of where they want to be in their careers beyond the next few years. They may also desire the flexibility to adjust to changes in the employment marketplace and the evolution of new opportunities. The decision on the long- versus short-term view can also be influenced by the stage of your career. Early in your career, you may want to take the long-term view because of the many years you have in front of you. Later in your career, you may want to take a short-term view because you have fewer years until retirement. Success will come from the focus that results from setting a period of time.

Once you have set a period of time for developing your product, focus on designating your target position. An excellent source of information for setting your target are individuals who are experienced in the discipline you want to pursue (finance, marketing, information technology, sales, manufacturing, logistics, et al.). Approach your current or former supervisors, peers, mentors, and/or executives with whom you are connected.

A target position should include the following components:

- Responsibilities
- Qualifications
- To whom the position will report
- Role of the position in the company or organization
- Key attributes or traits required for the position
- Compensation
- Location
- Travel

By establishing the position you want to target, you can focus your time and resources on researching what the employment market requires for the position. Again, individuals who are experienced in the discipline you want to pursue can provide information on what the position requires. You can also gather information by visiting Internet job sites such as CareerBuilder and Monster, your current employer's website, and websites of other companies. Do not minimize or overlook the importance and benefits of researching sources other than those of your current employer. Information from external resources is based on a broader view of the employment marketplace. When you research external sources, you:

- Identify new and emerging techniques and competencies that may not be used by your current employer. Your company may seek candidates in the future who are skilled in these techniques and competencies instead of training current employees (including you). These new employees—your competitors—would get the position that you targeted.
- Discover career opportunities or options beyond your current employer. You may identify opportunities to develop your product to fit a broader market (in this case, potential employers, including those who are willing to pay a higher price for your product—your skills and capabilities).

Developing Your Personal Product Concept

Your Target Position Description, complete with information for each component, is your personal product concept for satisfying what your market requires. Your market is the people or employers who can hire, promote, or pay you more for your skills and capabilities. You establish the vehicle to create value when you offer a product that satisfies the requirements of your market. Your target position description includes the components described above.

The Responsibilities component of the Target Position Description should include accountabilities and scope. Accountabilities establish why the position will exist. Accountabilities include:

- Activities or functions that you will manage or supervise or to which you will be assigned.
- Services and/or capabilities the position is responsible for providing to the company or its customers.

Scope establishes the limits of the responsibilities of the position. It should include:

- Number of employees reporting to the position.
- Number of locations for which the position will be responsible.
- Geography (regions of the country or world for which the position will be responsible for supporting).

You should state the number of employees you expect to manage in a range rather than an exact number. The number of employees you expect to manage will indicate how much supervisory experience and training you will need.

The number of locations should be specified as single or multiple, rather than as an exact number. Responsibilities spanning more than one location will indicate the need to manage *without a physical presence.* No one can be in more than one place at a time. As responsibilities grow beyond one location, individuals will need to acquire or improve communications, organizational, relationship management, and other skills that enable their effectiveness in multi-location organizations.

Geography is an important factor for many companies in today's business environment. Companies that operate or seek to operate globally will seek candidates who have experience working in or with operations in different regions of the world. In some cases, companies pay a premium for global experience.

Split qualifications into two categories—required and preferred. Required qualifications are those that you *must* have to be considered as a candidate for your target position. Preferred qualifications are those that are *desired*—but not required—for consideration. For example, your research may reveal that in-depth knowledge of SEC reporting rules and a CPA are requirements for a director of corporate accounting in the financial services sector and an MBA with a concentration in finance or accounting is preferred. Categorizing qualifications as required or preferred will help you prioritize your personal product development efforts (make achievement of required qualifications your top priority).

Components of the Qualifications component of your Target Position Description should include the following elements:

- Experience
- Number of years of experience
- Type of experience

- Progression of experience
- Education
- Certifications

Number of years of experience should also be stated as a range (e.g. three–five years) rather than an exact number.

Type of experience could include combinations of experiences within your discipline as well as other disciplines. For example, your research could reveal that the market is requiring that corporate accounting directors have experience within accounting in areas such as financial reporting, tax, and audit, as well as experience outside of accounting in areas such as implementing financial systems. Requirements for marketing directors could include experience within marketing such as promotions management, advertising, and product management, as well as experience in sales. If your target position is Chief Information Officer (CIO), your research of the market may reveal a need for experience within information technology such as solutions development and infrastructure management, as well as business consulting experience.

For individuals who are seeking their first job, taking a job with companies that are respected for their development of talent in certain disciplines (marketing, finance, information technology management, et al.) will increase their future marketability in the employment marketplace. Some companies will seek individuals who have experience with companies known for developing people in certain disciplines and paying a premium to hire those individuals into management and executive positions. I witnessed this practice when I worked in a consumer packaged goods business unit of a diversified manufacturing company. Individuals joining the marketing function after graduating from universities could advance to the position of assistant product manager. However, the company hired individuals into the position of product manager from companies known for their leadership in product management. This included companies such as Procter & Gamble, Kraft/General Foods, and Gillette.

Progression of experience is the *professional ladder* you should climb to be a competitor for your target position. For example, your research may reveal that the position of division controller in a manufacturing company may require a climb up the professional ladder from accountant to analyst to manager to plant controller to manager of financial planning and analysis.

Your research may also reveal the need for experience managing budgets. In some cases, a job posting may reveal an estimate of the level of annual budget responsibility for which your target position could be responsible.

Identifying the person to whom your target position reports may indicate a need to develop certain interaction skills. Your effectiveness will require differences in approaches to, and interactions with, a senior level position (CEO or someone who reports to the CEO) versus individuals at lower levels. You can seek the advice of a mentor, an executive to whom you are connected, or a coach to advise you on how to approach and interact with people at different levels.

Including the role of the position in the company or organization in your Target Position Description will indicate the types of experience or exposure that you should include in your personal development. For example, your research may reveal that the marketing director position that you are targeting may require building an effective relationship with the sales department. This may point to the need to take an assignment in sales, or having occasional discussions and exchanges with individuals in the sales organization, especially individuals who have extensive knowledge and experience in sales.

Individuals who make hiring and promotion decisions know that being effective in a position includes having certain attributes and traits that go beyond qualifications. For example, positions may require being innovative, a problem-solver, an organizer, or being detail-oriented. If your research of the market reveals that the attributes and traits of the position you have targeted do not match your strengths, you should change your target position. For example, you may find that your strengths are more suitable for a staff or support position than for being the leader of a function (e.g. senior tax consultant rather than director of taxes). One of the benefits of *The Business of Me* Process is matching what you offer (your product) to those who will buy it (hire or promote you).

Compensation is the value the market assigns to your product—your skills and capabilities. Job postings often reveal salary ranges for positions. When you research compensation, you are conducting your *personal salary survey*. You get an idea of your value. You may also discover features that you can add to your product to increase its value or asking price. For example, researching information technology positions may reveal that the marketplace assigns a higher value to positions requiring Project Management Professional (PMP) certification versus those that do not require the certification. The investment in training may be $1,000, but the annual salary *premium* may be $3,000. *Seeking to maximize the value of your product, would you invest $1,000 to realize an annual income stream of an additional $3,000?*

Your research has revealed the responsibilities, qualifications, key attributes, and other market requirements for your target position. Your research of compensation established its value. What about managing the balance between your work and your personal life? This is known as the *work/life balance*. Personal issues in the *life* component can impact your effectiveness in the *work* component and vice versa. The responsibilities, qualifications, key attributes, and compensation make up the *work* component of the balance. The location and travel components of your target position can impact the *life* component of your work/life balance.

In terms of location, your research may reveal that your best opportunities are located primarily in a geographical location other than where you currently reside. You may need to consider the need to relocate as you make decisions related to home purchases and investments, as well as the trade-offs between family and professional life. For example, how do your spouse and children feel about relocation? How would relocation impact your involvement in community activities? Will the compensation or value assigned to the position relative to the cost of living for the location allow you to improve or maintain your standard of living if you relocated?

Job posting may state the travel related to the position. Travel is often stated in the percentage of time the employee will be required to be away from the office. It should be considered in your ability to balance work with family and other components of your personal life.

Following is an example of a Target Position Description:

Target Position Description
Virginia Billings

Title
Director of Corporate Accounting

Responsibilities
- Accountabilities: Direct financial planning and analysis for global manufacturing corporation
    o Plan and manage annual budgeting process
    o Direct development of quarterly corporate earnings and cash flow forecasts
    o Plan and lead quarterly reviews of operating results and financial position with Corporate Executive Committee
    o Provide analysis of trends for quarterly disclosures and discussions with investment community
    o Ensure maintenance of world-class financial systems by leading Financial Systems Quality Review Team
    o Support development of talent to ensure continuous stream of effective financial managers
- Scope
    o Manage team of 7–10 financial professionals
    o Serve as point of coordination for global financial organizations

Qualifications
- Required
    o Bachelor's degree in Accounting
    o Certified Public Accountant
    o Five years of Big 4 Public Accounting experience
    o Progressive experience from entry-level financial analyst to manager of financial planning and analysis for major business group within Fortune 500 company

- o Two–three years of experience developing budgets at corporate level
- o Experience presenting to executives
- o Experience implementing financial reporting component of leading Enterprise Resource Planning system
- o Excellent oral and written communications skills
- o Proficiency in Microsoft PowerPoint
- Preferred
  - o MBA with concentration in Finance or Accounting
  - o Experience implementing financial reporting component of SAP
  - o Two years as leader of client delivery team in Big 4 Public Accounting firm

To Whom Position Reports
Position reports to Vice President and Corporate Controller. Corporate Controller reports to Senior Vice President and Chief Financial Officer (CFO). CFO reports to Chief Executive Officer (CEO).

Role of Position in Company
Position serves as the point of coordination for development for all corporate financial planning and analysis activities. It provides the information for communications relating to the financial status of the company to senior management and the investment community. Information must be accurate and timely. Position is also the focal point for ensuring that company utilizes best-in-class financial reporting systems.

Key Attributes and Traits
- Analytical, probe beyond what is given
- Relationship-builder who can establish trust with peers and company executives
- Confident, comfortable presenting unfavorable news to senior management
- Self-starter who will take action to initiate process improvements

Compensation
* Base salary: $120,000–$150,000
* Bonus: 25–40%

Location
Major metropolitan area

Travel
15%

Again, your Target Position Description is your product concept, the basis for developing your prototype. Your prototype translates the requirements of your Target Position Description into a model that captures what your product (skills and capabilities) must provide to satisfy your target market (people who can hire, promote, and compensate you). Your prototype will establish the blueprint to develop your product.

Developing Your Prototype

The actions we take to address the challenges we face are often at our feet. Answers often come from shifts in the way we think. Before we delve into how to develop your prototype, take a deep breath and open your mind to think beyond how you currently use résumés.

Have you ever submitted your résumé for a position and thought, *"I wish that I had more of that experience, education, or training; earned that certification; or participated in Project XYZ that would have provided the opportunity to strengthen my candidacy for this position"?* How can you avoid these "I wish I had" statements? The prescription I recommend is the Pro Forma Résumé. The Pro Forma Résumé is the résumé you want to submit when you apply for your Target Position. It is your *prototype.* It will capture what you will have to offer to your target market—the individuals who can hire, promote, and compensate you.

Pro Forma Résumés are similar to the projected, or pro forma financial statements that companies submit to investors and bankers to predict how well their companies will perform if they receive the funding they request. Just as pro forma financial statements set performance expectations for businesses, the Pro Forma Résumé sets the expectations for the value your personal product could provide.

Your Pro Forma Résumé is the tool that you use to design your product. It defines the details of the product (skills and capabilities) that you will develop for your target market. These details include additional training and education, certifications, and experience. It also provides the criteria for determining which assignments and positions you need to pursue to develop your product.

Keep in mind that the Pro Forma Résumé differs from the traditional résumé. Résumés are traditionally used to state what individuals have accomplished and their qualifications (experience, education, skills, certifications, et al.). The traditional résumé is *what you are*. The Pro Forma Résumé is *what you want to be or what you are striving to be*.

Your Pro Forma Résumé should include the following components:

- Career Summary
- Career Highlights
- Professional Experience
- Education
- Training and Certifications
- Memberships and Affiliations

Your Career Summary should communicate your *Personal Brand Statement*. Your Personal Brand Statement communicates what you stand for, the value you offer, and what makes you unique. We will cover the development of personal brand statements in chapter two.

Career Highlights should include three to five significant accomplishments that you want to achieve to qualify you for your target position. (What types of accomplishments do positions similar to your target position require or would give you an advantage over your competitors for these positions?) You can establish these accomplishments by researching job postings similar to your target position on job sites. You can also determine the accomplishments you want to include in your Pro Forma Résumé through discussions with individuals who have achieved the position you want to achieve or are knowledgeable of your discipline (finance, marketing, information technology, et. al.).

Establishing what you want to accomplish will focus you on identifying and pursuing assignments that will strengthen your competitive position for your target position. For example, you could approach your boss or an executive in your organization with a project proposal that will satisfy a business or organizational need, while enabling your personal product development. Following are guidelines for developing your career highlights:

- State each accomplishment as a bullet point.
- Start each accomplishment (bullet point) with an action verb that represents the level of position that you are seeking. If you are seeking a position in management or as an executive, use verbs such as "led," "directed," "reduced," "implemented," and "increased."
- Avoid the use of passive phrases such as "participated in" or "was involved in." (You want to achieve—not just be exposed to the achievements of others.)
- Express the results as:
  o Benefits your organizations or companies will realize as a result of your actions. (Quantify the benefits. This could also focus you on pursuing opportunities that will provide the experience you want to have—those XYZ projects that will keep you from being a victim of *I wish I had*.)
  o Actions you will take to generate the benefits.

Professional Experience is the positions and assignments on your *professional ladder* that we discussed in the Progression of Experience component of your Target Position Description. The professional experience you want to acquire should also consider the responsibilities, qualifications, to whom the position will report, and the role of positions components of your Target Position Description.

The education, training and certifications, and membership and affiliations components of your Pro Forma Résumé should also be based on the content of these components in your Target Position Description.

Following is an example of a Pro Forma Résumé for a financial professional who is seeking to become a director of corporate accounting for a global manufacturing corporation. The Pro Forma Résumé is based on the Target Position Description the individual developed.

Pro Forma Résumé
Virginia Billings

Career Summary

Accounting and Finance professional manager who has contributed to significant increases in organizational profits and effectiveness. Noted for ability to identify and articulate factors driving financial results, providing clear direction to financial teams, communicating effectively with senior executives, building relationships, and developing talent. In-depth understanding of the accounting and finance function gained through experience from entry level to middle management.

Career Highlights

- Contributed to 25% growth in operating profit for $1 billion business unit by implementing improvements that increased the accuracy and timeliness of quarterly profit forecasts.
- Reduced period closing cycle from 10 to 5 days by leading the implementation of the financial reporting components of SAP.
- Enabled 5 percentage point profit margin improvement for product group by obtaining senior management approval of new value-added analysis technique.
- Eliminated financial reporting audit issues requiring senior management review for $5 billion corporation.
- Supported success of succession planning process by coaching and mentoring the development of two functional accounting managers for corporate controller group.

Professional Experience

Senior Manager, Public Accounting   2000–2006
Advanced from entry-level auditor to senior manager in four years. Led audit teams responsible for the certification of annual financial statements for Fortune 500 client. Managed team of seven auditors.

Manager, Financial Planning and Analysis   2006–2008
Managed preparation of annual budgets and quarterly profit forecasts for $1 billion business unit. Planned and coordinated monthly operations reviews with business unit senior management team. Led cross-functional teams focused on improving business unit profitability. Managed staff of eight professional analysts.

Manager, Financial Reporting   2008–2010
Led consolidation of monthly, quarterly, and annual corporate financial statements for Fortune 500 company. Ensured that statements complied with SEC reporting rules. Served as point of contact between external auditors and corporate finance functions and controller groups for business units. Led implementation of financial reporting component of SAP. Managed staff of seven professional accountants.

Education
MBA, Accounting, State University, 2004
BS, Accounting, State University, 2000

Training and Certifications
Certified Public Accountant
Subject Matter Expert, SAP Financial Accounting
Trained in *Pyramid Principle of Writing*
Proficient in use of Microsoft PowerPoint

Memberships and Affiliations
Member, AICPA
Member, State University School of Accountancy Alumni Board

Developing Your Product

Your Personal Product Development Plan is your Professional Development Plan. That plan includes the actions and steps that you will take to *transform* your *Pro Forma Résumé* into your *actual* résumé—your path from *possibility to reality*.

Transformation, moving from possibility to reality, is a frequent need for companies. The need to transform may be driven by changes in the marketplace, changes in technology, or the need to change the way companies produce, market, and deliver their products. Transformation includes five basic steps:

1. Establish the Desired State. (What does the organization want to be?)
2. Assess the Current State. (Where is the organization now relative to the Desired State?)
3. Determine what is keeping the organization from being what it can be.
4. Determine actions the organization needs to take to transform.
5. Execute the transformation.

You can use these five steps to enable your personal transformation.

Business Transformation	Career Transformation
Desired State	Pro Forma Résumé
Current State	Current Résumé (Traditional Résumé)
What is keeping the organization from being what it can be?	Gaps between Current and Pro Forma Résumé: Problems, Challenges, Needs to be Satisfied
Actions	Personal Product Development Plan (Career/Professional Development Plan)
Execution	Close Gaps

Again, your Pro Forma Résumé is what you want to be or what you are striving to be. Your current or traditional résumé is what you are.

You can use the following diagrams to enable your career transformation. The first diagram illustrates the execution of steps 1 and 2 of a personal transformation process. The target position is director of accounting.

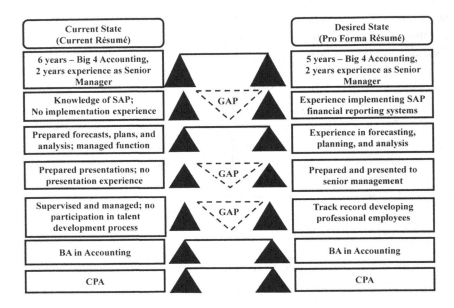

Gaps are the things that must be developed or acquired to reach the Desired State.

Now, let's illustrate Step 3—what keeps individuals from being what they can or want to be.

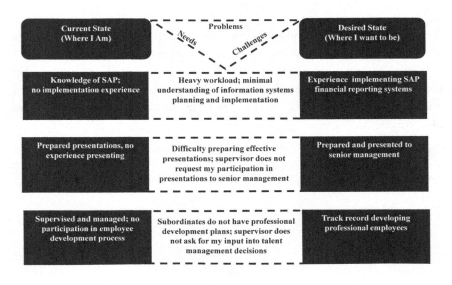

Following is an example of how to accomplish steps 4 and 5 of the Career Transformation Process—determine actions to enable the transformation and execute the actions to close the gaps.

- Heavy workload
  - o Take management course to enable more effective use of time
  - o Learn how to use time-management tools
  - o Delegate more to staff
- Minimal understanding of information systems planning and implementation
  - o Read information on information systems planning and implementation or take a course focused on systems planning and implementation
  - o Attend information systems vendors' briefings and educational events
  - o Seek assignment to systems implementation project team
  - o Seek developmental assignment in information systems
  - o Develop relationships with information technology professionals to learn about systems planning and implementation
- Difficulty preparing effective presentations
  - o Take a course to improve public speaking and presentation skills
  - o Master use of PowerPoint
- Supervisor does not ask me to participate in or attend presentations to senior management
  - o Establish relationship with a senior manager or someone who interacts with senior management to gain insight into presenting to senior executives
  - o Take steps to gain the confidence of supervisor, such as providing additional information to enhance his/her presentations
- Subordinates do not have professional development plans
  - o Prepare your personal professional development plan, share it with your supervisor, and market the benefits of personal development planning to your subordinates (this will demonstrate your interest in developing staff)

- Supervisor does not ask for input into planning the professional development of your subordinates
    - o Instead of waiting to be asked for your input, volunteer it, sharing your thoughts and opinions with your supervisor on developing employees
    - o Gain a sound understanding of the process for developing subordinates and link it to other personnel management activities for which you are responsible, such as performance reviews.

By applying the business process to develop your personal product development process, you can navigate your career from where you are today to where you want it to be. You will have the résumé that you want to submit when you apply for your target position.

Summary: Develop Your Product

Structure

1. Assess your strengths and capabilities.
2. Establish your target position.
3. Prepare your Target Position Description.
4. Develop your Pro Forma Résumé.
5. Make transformation from where you are to where you want to be in your career.

Filing Cabinet

Situation/Need	Information on File
Establishing a career development plan	• Strengths • Skills and capabilities • Employment market opportunities • Development target (Target Position Description) • Personal Development Prototype (Pro Forma Résumé) • Experience, training, and certification needs • Process for developing career plan
Planning a job search	• Information for résumé • Personal salary survey • Target Position Description to focus job search
Preparing a résumé	• Strengths • Skills and capabilities • Key career accomplishments
Preparing for interviews	• Strengths • Skills and capabilities • Key career accomplishments

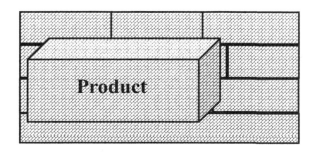

Chapter 2:

Brand Your Product: Make Yourself Unique

"You're hired, you report to work, you join a team—and you immediately start figuring out how to deliver value to the customer. Along the way, you learn stuff, develop your skills, hone your abilities, and move from project to project. And if you're really smart, you figure out how to distinguish yourself from all the other very smart people walking around in $1,500 suits, with high-powered laptops, and well-polished résumés. Along the way, if you're really smart, you figure out what it takes to create a distinctive role for yourself—you create a message and a strategy to promote the brand called You."

—Tom Peters, "The Brand Called You," *Fast Company Magazine*

29

Why hire or promote me instead of others?

Product Branding: Business Management Process

Imagine an aisle in a grocery store stocked with paper towels on the shelves. As you walk through the aisle, you notice that all the paper towels are simply marked *Paper Towels*. There is no way to distinguish one package of paper towels from the next. Consumers could pick any one of the packages at random, basing their decision on factors such as location of the paper towel on the shelf and price. Consumers could take their selection home and try it, and if they are pleased with it, they could return to the store, hoping to find the same paper towels as before. However, because there is no real way to distinguish one package of paper towels from the next, purchasers could only hope that they selected the one with the same features and capabilities as the paper towel they purchased during their previous trip to the store. That would be some purchasing experience!

Now, keeping this in mind, think of the manufacturer. All the product development efforts to provide a product that satisfies the needs of its target market would be lost, making theirs just another paper towel among many on the shelf.

Companies establish brands to distinguish their products. Brands present images of how companies want customers to perceive their products and provide *a reason to buy* their products. Brands communicate:

- What the brand stands for.
- The value the brand offers.
- What makes the brand unique.

Following are examples of brand images.

Brand	Image	Message
Coca-Cola	*The Real Thing*	This is the original. This is the standard for colas. There is no substitute.
Bounty	*The Quicker Picker Upper*	You can remove that spill quickly and with no hassle.
Ivory	*99 & 44/100% Pure*	There is nothing in this soap that will harm you.

Famous people are also branded:

Person	Image	Message
Joe DiMaggio	*The Yankee Clipper*	Athlete's standard for class, dignity, and grace.
Ronald Reagan	*The Great Communicator*	Relates to me. Makes it plain and simple.
Reggie Jackson	*Mr. October*	Delivers when it counts the most.

The Product Branding component of the Business Management Process includes the following steps:

1. Define strengths.
2. Define the values the brand represents.
3. Define the value the brand offers.
4. Identify what makes the brand unique.
5. Establish a model for projecting the desired image.
6. Articulate the value the brand offers.
7. Deliver the value that the brand promises.

Product Branding: *The Business of Me*

You can apply the concept of branding to provide your customers—your potential or current employers—with a reason to hire or promote you. Just like brands offered by companies, your personal brand will communicate:

- What you stand for: What do you want people to think or say when they see you or hear your name?
- The value you offer: What skills and capabilities can you provide to your current and potential employers?
- What makes you unique: How do you distinguish yourself from your competitors?

By reading this chapter, you will:

1. Gain an understanding of why it is important to establish your personal brand.
2. Be introduced to a process for developing your brand.
3. Learn how to communicate the benefits of your brand to people who can hire, promote, or compensate you.
4. Be alerted to resources and tools to enable the development of your personal brand.

Let's apply the steps of the Product Branding component of the Business Management Process to the development of your personal brand.

Define Your Strengths, Values, and the Value You Offer

In chapter one, we discussed the importance of knowing our strengths to enable our professional development and to increase the value that we can provide. The strengths that you define help you identify situations, roles, and assignments in which you will be at your best. In the case of Personal Branding, our strengths provide a foundation for developing the image we want to create and project. Applying a business example of building on strengths, the makers of Bounty build on the strength of the product to quickly absorb spills. That strength is communicated to potential customers through the brand identity. That identity is embedded in the *Quicker Picker Upper* message.

Our values are who we are. Our values embody our beliefs and principles—the things that drive our behavior. Values are reflected in behaviors such as:

- Leading
- Creating
- Contributing
- Relating
- Teaching

There are assessments that can help you confirm your values and rank your personal values in the order of your most to least dominant. You can use values assessment tools that are available on the Internet. You can identify assessments by using values assessments as keywords for your search. You can also consult with a coach or career counselor who will then be able to help you evaluate and apply the results of your assessment.

As you develop your personal product and make the transformation to make your Pro Forma Résumé a reality, you will gain experience and have opportunities to make contributions that demonstrate the value you can offer.

Identify What Makes You Unique

You can determine what makes you unique through multiple sources, including:

- Input from peers, colleagues, and current and former supervisors
- Performance appraisals and evaluations
- Your *finest moments*

When seeking input from your peers, colleagues, and supervisors, consider asking questions such as:

- What descriptions or adjectives come to mind when you see me, hear my name, or think of me?
- In what types of situations would you ask for my participation or help?
- In what situations am I at my best?

You can also receive input into determining what makes you unique by participating in 360-degree feedback surveys. These surveys are assessments that provide feedback from your superiors, peers, and subordinates on how you are perceived. If your company does not offer 360-degree surveys, you can conduct your own. Several feedback surveys are available on the Internet at no-to-minimal cost. Search the Internet for survey tools using keywords such as "360-degree," "multi-rater feedback," "multi-source feedback," and "multi-source assessment."

Reviewing performance appraisals and evaluations can reveal recurring themes or comments about traits and strengths that make you unique.

The things that define you can become evident in your *finest moments*—those situations and events when you excelled and overcame adversity and challenges. List your most satisfying accomplishments and then list what actions you took, or characteristics you displayed, in order to achieve your goal. Following are examples of labels that could capture your uniqueness:

- Problem-solver
- Organizer
- Stabilizer
- Ms./Mr. Reliable
- Innovator
- Influencer
- Team-builder
- Thought leader

By making such a list, you will begin to notice common themes and traits, helping you define what makes you unique and valuable. You can also use your list to compare the terms to the results of assessments of your strengths that you performed as you developed your product. A coach or career counselor can also assist you in establishing the labels that reflect your uniqueness.

Establish Your Personal Image Model

You have probably heard someone say, "I may not be able to tell you exactly what I want, but I will know it when I see it." Establishing a model for demonstrating your personal brand image will help others *see it* in you. An effective way to establish your model is to develop it based on the image projected by individuals who have achieved what you are seeking. Consider the following questions:

- What comes to your mind when you see or think of them?
- What makes them unique?
- What words would you use to describe them?

Observe how these individuals:

- Present themselves to others
- Communicate
- Interact with others
- Dress
- Work and operate

These individuals have been successful in their organizations because they fit the *cultures* of their companies. Culture is the company's personality; it includes how individuals work, how things get done, how individuals act, and acceptable behaviors and norms. By developing your model based on already successful people within your company or your desired company, you can develop your personal success model. Focus on how you present yourself, communicate, interact with others, dress, and operate based on your personal image model. Seek feedback from peers, friends, and others who work with you or observe you in the workplace. See if these traits are included in the results of feedback surveys or comments in your performance appraisals. If there are gaps between the feedback you receive and the image you want to project, seek the assistance of a coach or mentor to help you close the gaps.

Articulate the Value You Offer

Once you have defined your strengths and values, identified what makes you unique, and established a model to project your brand identity, you are positioned to communicate the value you can provide to individuals who can hire or promote you, increase your compensation, or who can influence individuals who make hiring, promotion, and compensation decisions. This expression of your value is captured in your Personal Brand Statement. Your Personal Brand Statement communicates what you stand for, the value you offer, and what makes you unique. Following are three examples of personal brand statements:

Personal Brand Statement 1

I am a focused and determined financial manager with entrepreneurial instincts. I translate trends and business indicators into opportunities to increase profits. I stand apart from my peers and colleagues in the corporate finance profession because of my ability to effectively communicate opportunities and concepts to business partners who are not financial professionals. Because of these traits, my organization is able to move quickly to take advantage of opportunities in the marketplace.

Personal Brand Statement 2

I am a thought leader who can structure and package ideas, perspectives, and opinions from several sources into business concepts. I also have the ability to relate to business leaders and have the drive to accomplish daunting tasks. This enables the business units that I support to move beyond concepts and discussion to the development of action plans. The executives in my organization invite me to join in efforts to sort through large amounts of data.

Personal Brand Statement 3

> *I am a problem solver. I utilize my strong analytical skills, knowledge of information technology infrastructure, and my tenacity to stay focused on a problem to develop solutions that not only solve current problems but also provide flexibility to adapt to the ever-changing information technology landscape.*

Note how each of the examples reflects strengths, values, and uniqueness.

What would you say if someone asked you, "What do you do?" This simple question might be overwhelming. So, how can you get people interested in hearing about you? Let's view this challenge using the following example.

> You are a senior financial executive attending a conference for accounting and finance professionals, hoping to identify *difference makers*, individuals who can increase the effectiveness of your organization and who can be developed to someday lead your organization after you have retired or moved on to bigger and better things. It is the social hour, you are standing with a drink in your hand, and you are a *magnet* that attracts the professionals. They are attempting to position themselves close to you for the opportunity to engage in a conversation with you. You ask several individuals the question "What do you do?" Their answers are driving you to consider removing your name tag, which identifies you as a senior executive (putting yourself out of your misery). You hear answers such as:

> *I perform financial analysis.* (That's it, nothing else. The person moves on when they see you attempting to make eye contact with someone else.)

> *I analyze financial results, prepare reports, and make presentations to management.* (So does everyone else in this room.)

> *I coordinate the budgeting process, which includes establishing the budget calendar, issuing instructions, consolidating*

budgets, and presenting budget proposals to management. (He is a busy beaver, making a lot of money, but I need designers, not bricklayers.)

You have encountered a lot of *paper towels* but no difference makers. As you look for a waiter to take your empty glass, you ask one more person the question "What do you do?" The person responds:

I identify opportunities to improve the performance of my company.

The person has sparked your curiosity. You want to know more.

Executive: *How do you do that?*
Professional: *I translate data—such as profits, margins, and market shares—into trends and relationships.*

The executive is now really focused on the individual who senses the executive's curiosity and his thirst for more information. He continues:

I present this information in state-of-business summaries that provide implications and identify opportunities.

The executive is really thirsty. He asks *"How do you facilitate decision making?"* The professional replies:

I link details to the key points of the summary with the advantages and disadvantages of each opportunity.

The executive responds:

Here is my business card. Call my office next Tuesday. My assistant will schedule a continuation of our discussion. Do you have a copy of your résumé or a business card?

I am sure that this is the type of conversation we all would like to have with someone who could hire us into a great career opportunity. Why did the executive continue his discussion with this particular professional but not the others? It was because the professional communicated several key items in concise statements:

- Strengths (ability to translate data into useful information)
- Values (creating and contributing)
- Uniqueness (standing out versus peers)

Your personal brand statement is also known as an *elevator speech*. In business, an elevator speech is a brief and concise statement (so named because it can be used during an elevator ride) of an idea, product, service, project, or initiative that:

- Defines the product, service, project, or initiative
- Communicates the value it will provide to the potential customer
- Differentiates the product from those offered by the competition

Following are considerations for developing and articulating your personal elevator speech:

- Establish *what* before talking about *how* something is done. (Adhere to the *Law of Sausage Making*. People love the taste of sausage. However, many people would not eat sausage if they knew how it is made!)
- Know your value. You exist in your organization or company to bring value. The more value you provide, the more distinctive you become and the greater your opportunities for advancement. But remember, value is in the eyes of the beholder. State your value in a manner to which your audience can relate. This includes the problems they have—the things that consume their attention. (Marketing professionals refer to these problems as the *pain* the audience is experiencing.)

Deliver the Value Your Brand Promises

You purchase a battery for your car. The manufacturer claims, "*Starts the first time, every time.*" You attempt to start your car, and it ends up taking five turns of the ignition key, not one, to get your car to start. What would be your opinion of the battery manufacturer?

The strength of your personal brand is determined by your delivery of the value that you say you offer. This is your brand promise. Remember that actions speak louder than words. Individuals are hired or promoted based on convincing decision makers that they can provide value—solve problems presented by the opportunity, satisfy the needs of the organization, or contribute to the accomplishment of the organization's goals and objectives. If you were a decision maker, how would you feel if, after hiring someone, that person did not provide what was promised? Your response to this situation could be firing or demoting the individual. As the individual, you would not be viewed as a *value creator*. That is why it is important for you to back your brand promises with the delivery of the results you promised or your customer expected (your customers being your supervisors and employers). We will address setting and delivering on expectations in chapter five.

Summary: What, When, How

Structure

1. Define your strengths.
2. Define your values.
3. Define the value you can offer.
4. Identify what makes you unique.
5. Establish a model for projecting your image.
6. Articulate the value you offer and what makes you unique.
7. Deliver the value that your brand promises.

Filing Cabinet

Situation/Need	Information on File

Preparing a résumé	• Personal Brand Statement
	    o Your values
	    o Value you offer
	    o What makes you unique

Interviewing for position or assignment	• Personal Brand Statement • Personal Elevator Speech
Projecting an image	• Personal Image Model • Feedback from surveys, peers, and others who observe you in the workplace
Attending conferences, networking, having discussions with hiring decision makers	• Personal Brand Statement • Elevator Speech
Deciding whether to accept a job offer in another company or organization	• Your values
Performing self-assessments for input into talent evaluations conducted by the management of your organization	• Value you offer • What makes you unique

Your Personal Brand: What You Stand for, What You Offer, What Makes You Unique

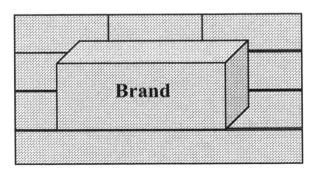

42

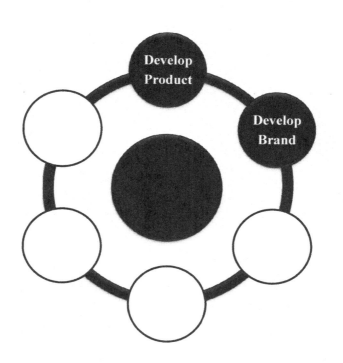

Section II

Get Your Value in Gear
- Market: Let Them Know What You Can Offer
- Sell: Get Hired

Chapter 3:

Market: Let Them Know What You Can Offer

"First thing to do is let everyone know you are in the game. It's like when you get into a kid's swimming pool. You have to make a splash. The bigger the splash, the more people will want to know about what you are doing and the more successful you will be."
—Max Markson, agent and author of *Show Me the Money*

Are decision makers aware of what I can do?

Marketing: Business Management Process

The paper towel example in chapter two emphasized the importance of product branding. Thinking of the example, let's suppose that the company brands its paper towels but never provides any information on the benefits the product offered or where it could be purchased. I'm sure we would agree that getting customers to purchase the product would be quite a challenge, if not nearly impossible.

Companies use the *marketing process* to create awareness of their products and to communicate the benefits of purchasing them. The foundation for the contemporary marketing process was established in the 1950s with the introduction of the *4Ps of Marketing Concept*:

- Product
- Price
- Placement
- Promotion

Variations, refinements, and expansions of the concept have occurred over the years, but the basic concept of integrating these four components still drives the development and execution of marketing plans. Robert Moment, a renowned business strategist and author of *It Only Takes a Moment to Score*, expanded the 4Ps to 6Ps to demonstrate how entrepreneurs could market their products to create value. The 6Ps are as follows:

- Persona
- Packaging
- Positioning
- Presentation
- Promotion
- Passion

6Ps	Include
Persona	<ul><li>What the product or business is all about</li><li>Values of business or product</li><li>What differentiates the product or business from its competitors</li></ul>
Packaging	<ul><li>Characteristics and quality of product package</li><li>Support, guarantees, and other things the product or business offers</li></ul>
Positioning	<ul><li>Right place, right time, and with right people (people likely to purchase)</li></ul>
Presentation	<ul><li>Impression product makes on customers</li></ul>
Promotion	<ul><li>Making product's benefits, what it stands for, and what makes it unique known to customers</li></ul>
Passion	<ul><li>Enthusiasm and energy company has for the product</li></ul>

Marketing: *The Business of Me*

As the CEO of your *Business of Me*, you can apply the 6Ps to managing your career to create awareness of your personal brand. When you create awareness, you increase the chances of having potential customers (people who can hire or promote you) purchase your product (hire or promote you). When your value is known, you also reduce the likelihood of having your earnings or employment disrupted during times of downsizing or restructuring—you keep your most valuable asset, your career, in operation. By reading this chapter, you will:

1. Gain an understanding of the important role personal marketing serves in managing your career.
2. Become familiar with measures that you can use to create awareness of your capabilities and skills.
3. Learn about resources and ideas you can use to bring attention to the value you can offer.
4. Get ideas on how to influence how others perceive you, especially individuals who can hire and promote you.
5. Obtain considerations for determining what assignments and positions will work best for you.

Let's apply the 6Ps of Marketing (Persona, Packaging, Positioning, Presentation, Promotion, and Passion) to managing your career to create awareness of your personal brand and the value it offers.

Persona

Persona answers the questions:

*   Who *are* you?
*   What do you *stand for*?
*   What *value* do you offer?
*   What makes you *unique*?

51

If these questions sound familiar, it's because we addressed them in chapter two, "Brand Your Product." Once you develop your brand, you have to make sure that the people who matter (hiring and promotion decision makers) are aware of it.

Companies use messages to ensure that potential customers are aware of the persona of their brands. Following are suggestions for creating awareness of your persona:

- Develop a statement that reflects your beliefs and values and refer to it frequently to guide your decisions and actions.
- Identify a motivational quote from a respected person that reflects how you want to be perceived. Post it in a location where individuals entering your office or cubicle can read it.
- Develop and perfect the delivery of your elevator speech.

During my corporate career, I developed a statement and titled it *This I Believe*—a statement of my beliefs and values. I read this statement several times a week and included it in the folder of important documents that I carried with me throughout the day. Having this statement fresh in my mind allowed me to speak and interact with others in ways that reflected what I stood for.

Posting motivational quotes from a respected person relates you to that person and creates an image for you. For example, when I was working in Corporate America, I posted a quote on my wall titled *Attitude,* by Charles Swindoll, an author and religious leader renowned for emphasizing the importance of attitude in guiding our lives. Swindoll said, *"Life is 10 percent what happens to you and 90 percent how you react to it."*

This quote planted the seeds for the image I wanted to project. The comments that I received from feedback surveys from peers, superiors, and subordinates complimented me on my positive attitude. This image persuaded decision makers in my organizations to assign me to difficult projects and functions—assignments that allowed me to demonstrate the value I could provide to organizations.

You may encounter potential customers or individuals who can influence decisions to hire or promote you, encounters that may include the individuals asking you, *"What do you do?"* This is a great opportunity to create awareness of your brand. As covered in chapter two, an effective means of communicating what your brand offers is your elevator speech.

Perfect it and practice its delivery. Don't miss an opportunity to create awareness.

Packaging

Persona focuses on developing the image you want to project. How can you build on that image to influence individuals to hire or promote you? Companies address this challenge, building on the brand image to influence the purchase decision, by packaging what they offer to satisfy the needs of their customers. Packaging includes things that customers see as well as the benefits they will experience when they purchase the products. Things that are visible to the customer include the configuration of the product (box, cellophane wrapper, etc.). The benefits that the customer will experience include customer service, warranties, and guarantees. This combination of things that are visible and to be experienced is often referred to as the *whole package*.

You may have heard people described as "having the whole package," people who have that combination of skills, capabilities, strengths, traits, and attributes that match the needs of the organization. The process you can use to develop your whole package was covered in chapter one, "Develop Your Product." That process, the Transformation Process, includes:

1. Establishing your Target Position Description to define situations that will match your strengths, skills, and capabilities.
2. Developing your Pro Forma Résumé to guide your preparation for the situations you target.
3. Identifying gaps between where you are now versus where you want to be (your current versus Pro Forma Résumé).
4. Determining actions to close gaps.
5. Closing the gaps.

This is an advantage of using the *Business of Me* process to manage your career. You develop information in one component of the process that can be used in several other components. This optimizes your efforts and promotes consistency across many career management requirements and situations.

Positioning

Positioning is getting your package into situations in which you can excel. Simply put, positioning is being at the right place, with the right people, and at the right time.

The right place and the right people go hand-in-hand as they include culture and environment, constantly influencing one another. Individuals thrive when they are working in a culture that enables them to use their strengths, skills, and capabilities in a manner that fits their traits and style. The compatibility between your traits and style and the traits and styles of people with whom you interact is referred to as *personal chemistry*. You can take assessments to help you define your chemistry, including how you make decisions, how you process information, and how you view your environment. Widely used assessments include Myers-Briggs Type Indicator, DISC, and Hermann Brain Dominance. Taking these assessments will help you understand your input into the mixture when you interact with others. Assessments will help you recognize the *right place* and *right people*. There are career counselors and coaches who can administer these assessments. There may be members of the human resources department at your company who are qualified to administer these assessments at no cost to you.

An excellent example of positioning is that of Dwight Eisenhower, the thirty-fourth president of the United States. Over the years, I have referred to it as the *Eisenhower Theory* as people with whom I had discussions said, "If I knew that this position would involve so many challenges and issues, I would not have accepted it." The Eisenhower Theory states that *Dwight Eisenhower would never have been president of the United States if it were not for World War II.*

Dwight Eisenhower was not promoted to the rank of brigadier general (one-star general, the lowest rank for generals) until October 1941, two months before Pearl Harbor and the entry of the United States into World War II. Several generals—Douglas MacArthur, George Patton, and Omar Bradley—held higher grades and had much more impressive résumés. Dwight Eisenhower, however, had that combination of interpersonal, leadership, and organizational skills needed to deal with the challenges presented by World War II—especially considering the conflicting personalities of General George Patton, Field Marshall Bernard Montgomery, Winston Churchill, and Charles de Gaulle and the requirement to get them to work together. World War II was the right time that enabled Dwight Eisenhower to use his skills, capabilities, and strengths to satisfy the needs presented by the war. As a consequence, he was appointed to lead the Allied forces in Europe and eventually rose to the rank of five-star general (the highest armed forces rank). Dwight Eisenhower's performance as Allied Commander positioned him to seek the nomination and to be elected president of the United States.

After having discussions with individuals who questioned their decision to accept a challenging assignment, most of them came to realize that the situations were opportunities to demonstrate what their brands offered. The situations were their *World War II opportunities.*

Presentation

How many times have you heard the expression *perception is reality?* Presentation creates perception. It is how we are seen by others. Individuals form opinions based on what they see. Your whole package will have minimal impact if it is not presented to individuals who decide or influence promotions, assignments, and compensation decisions in a manner that reflects your personal brand.

Presentation covers a wide spectrum of *viewpoints,* including your appearance, the way you interact with others, and the way you conduct business. Below are questions to ask yourself in determining how you are presenting yourself to others.

1. Are you dressing for the position to which you are aspiring instead of the position you have today? (If you want to look like a manager or executive, dress like one. Give others the opportunity to *see* you as a manager or an executive.)
2. Do you greet or interact with individuals in a manner that reflects your personal brand?
3. Do your work habits reflect your personal brand?
4. Do you *respond* or *react* to challenging situations and issues?
5. Do you perform and deliver results that meet, and at times exceed, the expectations of your manager and individuals, or departments that depend on you to accomplish their objectives?

6. What images do you present or value do you reflect when you participate in meetings?
7. Are you clear and concise when you speak?
8. Are your e-mail messages clear and concise, portraying your knowledge of the topic at hand?
9. Do attendees at your meetings compliment you on the way you conduct meetings, or do they avoid eye contact and conversations with you when your meetings end?
10. Do you present an image that you are in control of your career, know where you want to go, and are taking the actions to get you there?

Let's touch briefly on *responding* versus *reacting* to challenging situations and issues. Responding is *rational,* whereas reacting tends to be *emotional.* Emotions can create a fog, inhibiting your ability to present the image you desire others to see. Instead of creating a resolution for the problem at hand, your emotions become the focus, tarnishing your brand image—and may create additional issues for you to address. When you are rational, you deal with the situation at hand and do not create issues that you will have to deal with in the future.

Questions 5–10 are interactions that I refer to as *TouchPoints.* TouchPoints provide opportunities for you to demonstrate the value that you can provide to individuals who make or influence promotion and hiring decisions. I refer to these individuals as *career brokers.* Career brokers include:

- Your boss
- Your boss's boss
- Executives within your organization
- Peers of your boss
- The human resources representative who supports your organization
- Executives and other people of influence in your company

You can influence how career brokers perceive you by managing your TouchPoints. Your TouchPoints include:

- Your job performance
- How you participate in meetings
- Your communications (oral, written, electronic)
- How you conduct meetings

- How well you manage your career

Promotion

Companies also use promotion to convey the benefits of purchasing their products to potential customers. Once you have developed and branded yourself and you know the value that you can offer, it is critical that you promote your value to individuals who can decide or influence decisions to promote or hire you. Vehicles for self-promotion include:

- Networking
- Joining professional organizations
- Writing articles for publications
- Making presentations
- Participating in company-sponsored activities

Through networking, you can develop your *personal promotion organization*. If you connect with five people, who are connected with five people, who in turn are connected with five people, a hundred and twenty-five people become aware of the value that you can offer.

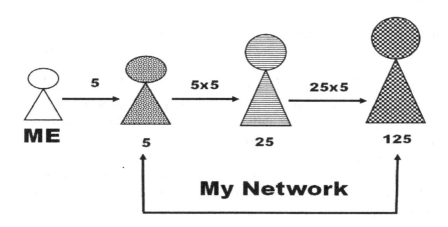

Become good at networking by reading articles and books on effective networking, as well as using resources such as your alumni association. I will provide more information on networking in chapter four, "Sell."

One of the keys to conducting effective promotions is promoting in the right places and at the right times. For example, beer companies advertise during televised professional football games because their target audience is men, and men are a large portion of the viewing audience for professional football. When soap operas started on television in the 1950s, their primary sponsors were companies that marketed laundry detergents and household cleaning products because the primary audience was housewives. Select occasions to network and make presentations, join professional organizations, and participate in events that include people who are connected to your target audience (people who may be interested in hiring or promoting you). Post your articles in periodicals and journals that your target audience reads or on Internet websites they visit.

Passion

Passion shines when we are at our best and doing things we enjoy. When you went through the Product Development Process, covered in chapter one, you positioned yourself to seek situations in which you could be successful and happy (right time, place, and people). Those situations were described in your *Target Position,* which was based on an assessment of your skills, capabilities, and strengths. When you develop your personal brand, you capture your values, what you offer, and what makes you unique. If you are honest with yourself in developing your target position, and target situations that align with them, your passion for your job will flow easily. However, if you are in a situation that you do not enjoy, you may attempt to present a *mirage of passion*, but the lack of passion will eventually overtake you, and your performance will eventually suffer.

To relate the importance of passion, I'd like to tell you about a colleague who had established an outstanding performance record in his business unit, flexing his strength and his passion—his analytical skills. In an attempt to broaden his experience, he accepted an assignment in the business unit in which I worked. The position involved financial transactions and support of day-to-day tactical activities. After a few weeks, it was clear that he was not performing well, and his coworkers and superiors could see he was not enjoying what he was doing, no matter how often he wore his *passion mask*. Within a few months, he returned to his previous business unit, was assigned to a role that utilized his strengths, and before long he returned to an outstanding level of performance. Through the years, he advanced to the top financial position in the unit, was promoted to general manager of the business unit, and when the company sold the business unit to another company, he was appointed president of the subsidiary the new company formed.

Summary: What, When, How

Structure

6Ps of Marketing:

- Persona
- Packaging
- Positioning
- Presentation
- Promotion
- Passion

Filing Cabinet

Situation/Need	Information on File
Developing and executing a career plan	Packaging, Positioning, Passion
Preparing a résumé	Persona, Packaging
Interviewing for position or assignment	Persona, Packaging, Positioning
Planning job search, career campaign	Packaging, Positioning, Promotion, Passion
Creating and sustaining personal image	Persona, Presentation
Influencing how you are perceived by superiors, peers, and subordinates	Presentation, Persona
Managing interactions with your career brokers	Persona, Packaging
Preparing your input into management reviews of organizational talent	Persona, Packaging
Considering job offers and assignments	Positioning, Passion, Persona
Building your personal network	Promotion

Marketing is letting everyone know you're in the game.

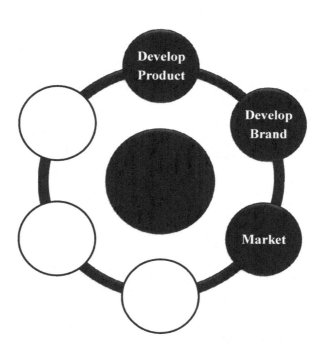

Chapter 4:

Sell: Get Hired

"Understand that you need to sell you and your ideas in order to advance your career, gain more respect, and increase your success, influence, and income."

—Jay Abraham, expert on business performance enhancement and author of *Getting Everything You Can Out of All You've Got*

How can I move from offering something to getting paid for what I offer?

Selling: Business Management Process

Companies sell their products through distribution channels. Distribution channels are the *paths* through which companies pass their products to their customers. For example, companies that offer consumer disposable products such as paper products, batteries, and snack foods may sell their products to consumers through grocery stores or through non-food outlets such as discount stores and drugstores. Regardless of the channel of distribution, companies sell their products by fulfilling the basic requirements of identifying leads, turning leads into prospects, and converting prospects into customers. These basic requirements can be expanded into the execution of following steps:

1. Identify leads
2. Qualify leads to determine prospects
3. Approach prospects
4. Present to prospects
5. Overcome rejection
6. Close
7. Follow up

Process Step	Focus
Identify leads	Identify potential customers—those who have needs the company's products could satisfy
Qualify leads	Determine *likely* customers (prospects) from population of *potential* customers (leads)
Approach prospects	Convince prospects to discuss the benefits the products offer
Present Prospects	Present products' benefits relative to the needs of prospects
Overcome rejection	Improve selling process by applying lessons learned from decisions of prospects not to purchase
Close	Offer terms and conditions of product purchase to prospects
Follow-up	Move prospects to customers by reaching agreement on terms and conditions

Selling: *The Business of Me*

By reading this chapter, you will:

1. Be introduced to a process that will move you from just having a product to getting value from it.
2. Become acquainted with a tool that will help you focus your personal selling efforts and increase the effectiveness of your networking.
3. Gain an understanding of the different paths to landing new career opportunities and how to migrate those paths.
4. Gain an understanding of how to capitalize on factors that govern hiring and promotion decisions within companies.
5. Get ideas on effective ways to approach and connect to individuals who can hire you or help you advance your career.

Now, let's apply the selling component of the Business Management Process to fulfill your need to persuade your current and potential employers to hire and/or promote you.

When you operate your *Business of Me*, you can sell your product (your skills and capabilities) through three primary channels:

- Referrals
- Applications to job postings
- Recruiting firms

"Searching the Hidden Job Market for Opportunities," an article in the April 1, 2008, edition of *CIO Magazine* estimated that 70–80 percent of new hires join their employers through personal connections or referrals. The article was written by Debra Feldman, a nationally recognized executive search consultant. Referrals are effective because they are built on *trust,* which results from building relationships with individuals who can connect you to hiring and promotion decision makers. Building trust involves three steps:

1. Know
2. Like
3. Trust

Networking is an effective way of executing the know step. It provides the opportunity for you to present or communicate your personal brand, as well as allowing people to become familiar with you. When people know you, they like you or become comfortable with you; in time, they will trust you. Once you have earned someone's trust, it will be more likely that they will refer you.

Applying to job openings includes responding to positions posted on Internet websites and openings advertised in newspapers, periodicals, and professional journals. Internet paths to job opportunities include popular career websites such as CareerBuilder, Monster.com, and My Career Space; company websites; and websites sponsored by professional organizations.

Applying for positions posted on websites is quick and convenient. You can apply for several openings in several locations in one day without leaving your computer. Because of the convenience of applying online, you may be one of hundreds, perhaps thousands, applying for the positions. Responding to the high volume of applications, companies have resorted to tactics such as the use of keyword software to screen résumés and applications, limiting the number of words applicants can use, and narrowing the scope of questions about the qualifications of applicants. The use of keywords for screening applications can be like engaging in a *guessing game.* What the employer is seeking and what you have may be an excellent match. However, the words that you use to communicate what you offer may just not be the exact words that the employer used to communicate the requirements.

The primary purpose of the screening process is to reduce the high volume of applications to a small number for referrals to decision makers. There is usually quite a distance in authority in companies between the persons responsible for performing the screening of applications and decision makers. Screening is a task often assigned to individuals at low levels of responsibility in human resources. Given this assignment, the process is usually designed to minimize the need for judgment on the part of the screeners. This reduces the flexibility of individuals to present their qualifications when they apply and the probability that their applications will progress beyond this early step in the hiring process.

Applying for positions online can also present privacy challenges to applicants. Many openings at career sites do not identify the company that has the opening. You do not know who is reading your application. You can imagine the unpleasant consequences of revealing to your employer that you are pursuing opportunities to leave the company.

Positions advertised in newspapers, periodicals, and professional journals present the same impersonal and privacy challenges that are presented by postings on websites. Responding to these advertisements requires more effort such as printing and mailing cover letters and résumés.

It is important to remember that recruiting firms (also known as search firms) are in the business of *finding people to fill positions*. Search firms are not in the business of *finding positions for people*. Although I do not recommend that you avoid them, I advise you not to rely heavily on them. Information on how to utilize recruiting firms will be covered in the *Identify Leads* step of the personal selling process.

Just like companies, you can apply the Business Management Selling Process regardless of the channel you are using to persuade your potential customers to purchase your skills and capabilities (hire you or advance your career). Again, these seven steps are:

1. Identify leads
2. Qualify leads to determine prospects
3. Approach prospects
4. Present to prospects
5. Overcome rejection
6. Close
7. Follow up

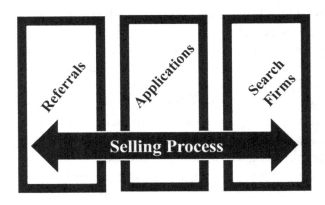

Identify Leads

Leads are potential prospects. In your case, potential prospects are organizations or companies that may offer hiring and promotion opportunities that match the benefits that your product offers. You identify potential prospects by relating your skills and capabilities to these situations.

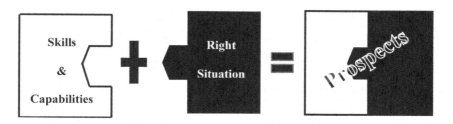

Your Target Position Description, covered in chapter one, "Develop Your Product," defines the *right situations*—industries and companies that could have needs that match what you offer. Your Target Position Description may even identify potential locations that offer opportunities. Below are two examples of identifying the right situations.

Example 1

An information technology professional has strong skills developing and implementing cost-effective solutions for managing computing operations in complex environments. Therefore, the professional could look for situations that present complexity, such as businesses with a diverse customer base (e.g., several segments in several regions of the world or from several sectors of the economy); companies that are planning on implementing or upgrading an Enterprise Resource Planning solution (ERP); or companies with environments in which quick response times are critical to the success of the business. The professional could also search for companies that are considering implementation of an information systems management solution of which she/he is very knowledgeable.

Example 2

> A certified public accountant with extensive knowledge and experience in Security and Exchange Commission (SEC) reporting requirements could search for companies that are moving from being privately held to having their stock listed on a stock exchange. In addition, an individual with this knowledge and certification could seek companies recently cited for violations of SEC financial reporting rules.

Unfortunately, ideal situations and opportunities won't just fall in your lap. You will need to actively search for situations that could match your skills and capabilities by:

- Reading periodicals, especially those focused on your area of expertise.
- Conducting Internet searches using keywords related to your skills and capabilities and situations that you are seeking—words included in your Target Position Description.
- Reviewing job postings on the Internet or in print media.
- Connecting with recruiting firms.
- Networking.

Let's discuss recruiting or search firms. As mentioned earlier, it is important to remember that search firms are in the business of finding people to fill positions—not finding positions for people. Following are suggestions that could help you establish relationships with search firms that could help you identify leads:

- Leverage connections that the search firm and you have in common. This will start you on the know/like/trust path to establishing a relationship with the firm.
- Make it easy for search firms to find you. Search firms rely on relationships. Network to create multiple points of connection to you to increase the likelihood that search firms will find you. This includes traditional points of contact such as peers, professional colleagues, and friends, as well as connections via the Internet such as LinkedIn and other social media avenues. Include your Personal Brand Statement in your social media profiles to broadcast the value you offer and what makes you unique.

- Be patient. After your initial contact with a search firm, let them initiate subsequent contacts with you unless there are developments or changes that may be of interest to the firm. This could include a promotion, significant change in responsibilities, job change, relocation, or change in your contact information. Time is a critical asset for search firms. They will contact you when there is a need to satisfy the needs of their customers.
- Refer potential candidates if a search firm contacts you requesting connections to candidates for positions for which you are not qualified or interested.
- Refer people that you know to search firms when the individuals are interested in making a connection. Keep in mind that search firms will form opinions of you based on the people with whom you associate. Therefore, make sure the people you refer will not damage your image. If the person who requests the referral is new to working with search firms, inform them about how search firms work.

Networking creates personal contacts who can serve as your *scouts* or points of connection to leads. Scouts can expand your search for leads from one (you) to many (possibly hundreds of individuals) who may be knowledgeable of situations that match your skills and capabilities. Establishing an effective network of scouts for identifying leads includes:

1. Creating awareness of your skills and capabilities
2. Creating awareness of your brand
3. Creating awareness of the types of opportunities you are seeking
4. Informing contacts of how they can help you
5. Informing contacts about how they can contact you

The traditional and most common method that individuals use to satisfy these requirements is providing résumés. Résumés touch on requirements 1, 2, and 5 through the career objectives, career summary, professional history, key accomplishments, and contact information components. However, résumés do not focus readers on the types of opportunities you are seeking—nor do they inform contacts of how they can help you.

Without this information, readers of your résumé are left to discern how they can help you.

A more effective method of employing your network to identify potential prospects is the use of the Personal Summary. The Personal Summary includes the following components:

- Career Summary
- Career Highlights
- Opportunities You Are Seeking
- Assistance You Need
- Contact Information

The *Career Summary* should communicate your personal brand. The Personal Brand Statement, covered in chapter two will provide the reference for crafting your career summary.

Career Highlights should include three-to-five of your major accomplishments. Express your accomplishments in bullet points, starting with action verbs in the past tense.

- Start accomplishments with action verbs that represent the level of position that you are seeking. If you are seeking a position in management or as an executive, use verbs such as "led," "directed," "reduced," "implemented," and "increased."
- Avoid the use of passive phrases such as "participated in" or "was involved in." Work is a problem to be solved. Solving problems takes more than being present at the time the problem is solved.
- Express the results as:
  o Benefits the organization realized as a result of your actions. (Quantify the benefits. Numbers speak loudly.)
  o Actions that you took to generate the benefits.
- Keep the statements concise—limit your accomplishments to a single sentence.

Review your *Career Summary* to ensure that it reflects the accomplishments that you include in your *Career Highlights*. Think like an attorney making her or his case. The Career Summary is the *opening argument*. Your Career Highlights are the *evidence*.

Next, connect your Career Summary and Career Highlights to the Opportunities You Are Seeking. Opportunities are the situations that could require your skills and capabilities—situations where you can add value. An illustration of this connection is presented in the Personal Summary example offered later in this section.

For the Assistance You Need component of your Personal Summary, express the types of connections you are seeking to help you identify leads. Connections can provide information that can help you focus your selling efforts as well as connect you to hiring decision makers or individuals who can influence decision makers. There are three types of connections you need—connections to individuals who:

- Are experiencing the problem
- Are knowledgeable of potential problems or of individuals experiencing the problem
- Serve or support those who have the problem

Of course, a connection to those who are experiencing the problem is the best assistance you could receive among the three types. Examples of those who are knowledgeable about potential problems include individuals who work or have worked in the situations or industries in which the problem often occurs. Examples of connections that serve or support those who have the problem include salespersons, suppliers, and consultants. Again, be brief. Limit the types of assistance to no more than five.

Contact information should include your e-mail address, telephone numbers (land and mobile), and home address.

Some individuals you contact may still request a résumé because they want more information—or because they are more comfortable with résumés than personal summaries. In those cases, provide the individual with hard and electronic copies of your résumé as well as your Personal Summary. Providing electronic copies will allow individuals to print as many hard copies as they need and also allow them to easily forward your information to individuals who may be able to help you. Following is an example of a Personal Summary.

Personal Summary
Catherine Smith

Career Summary

Leader and problem-solver who has implemented solutions that increased efficiency, effectiveness, and reliability of information systems infrastructure. Noted for solving complex problems, delivering projects on time and within budget, and for building strong relationships between information technology organizations and business partners.

Career Highlights

- Increased systems availability from 96% to 99.9% by leading the selection and implementation of systems management tools.
- Reduced supply chain systems service disruptions by 80% within six months by leading the integration of support systems between the company and its trade partners.
- Increased employee satisfaction with the computing environment from 60% to 90% and reduced systems disruptions by 60% by managing the implementation of the ITIL concept.
- Reduced annual software licensing costs by $800,000 by leading the implementation of an enterprise systems asset management solution.
- Strengthened partnership between Information Technology and end user community by introducing internal customer quality review boards.

Opportunities I Am Seeking

- Companies that are:
  - Considering or implementing an Enterprise Resource Planning solution (ERP).
  - Considering or implementing a systems management solution.
  - Operating in complex environments that require high systems availability, reliability, and quick response times.

- Consulting and systems integration firms that focus on designing and implementing systems management and/or ERP solutions.

How You Can Assist Me

- Alert me to opportunities.
- Identify individuals who may know individuals who:
    - Work for companies that may present opportunities.
    - Sell ERP and systems management solutions.
    - Work for consulting and systems integration firms that specialize in designing and implementing systems management solutions.
    - Belong to Information Technology professional organizations focused on infrastructure management.

How You Can Contact Me

E-mail address: cathsmith03@email.net
Telephone:
> Office: (999) 600-2000
> Mobile: (999) 600-9999
Home Address:
> 127 Mockingbird Lane
> Greenbriar, VA 23661

A Personal Summary reduces the guesswork for assisting you and allows individuals in your network to make efficient use of their time. It can be an essential component of your portfolio of personal selling materials. It also makes you stand out from those who are simply providing résumés.

Qualify Leads: Determine Prospects

The second step in the selling process is to qualify your leads. When you qualify leads, you determine:

- If the lead is a prospect.
- The best time to approach the prospect.

75

Your qualification of leads will glean *likely* customers (leads) from your list of *potential* customers (prospects). As a marketing coach advised me, qualifying customers separates the prospects (likely customers) from the suspects (potential customers). I suggest that you answer three questions to determine if a lead is a prospect:

1.   Does the lead recognize the problem?
2.   Is funding approved to hire someone to solve the problem?
3.   How difficult will it be to connect with the decision maker?

Let's pause to reflect on problems. Remember the formula we covered in "Identify Leads."

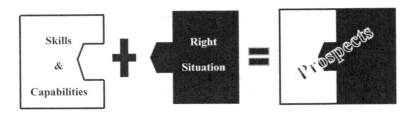

Work is a problem to be solved. Right Situations are problems—the needs that you satisfy. The research you performed and your networking to identify leads may have generated two types of opportunities—positions that are posted or advertised and opportunities that are not. The posting or advertising of the positions indicates a high probability that the problem is recognized and that funding has been approved to hire someone to solve the problem.

What about opportunities that are not posted or advertised? As stated earlier in this chapter, it is estimated that 70–80 percent of new hires join their new employers through personal connections or referrals. This occurs because many positions are not advertised. Given that qualifying leads in this large population of possibilities can consume a great deal of your effort, how can you optimize the use of your time and other resources? Let's answer questions 1 and 2. (Does the lead recognize the problem? Is funding approved to hire someone to solve the problem?)

What may appear to be an obvious problem to you may not be so obvious to the potential customer. For example, a problem may be *masked* by the daily heroic efforts of employees and not recognized by management or decision makers. Although these efforts will most likely be unsustainable, the problem may not be recognized by decision makers until it creates a significant incident or crisis. At that time, organizations will pay attention to the problem because of its consequences. Digging deeper into your research and seeking more detailed information from contacts in your network can reveal whether management and/or decision makers recognize the problem and what is causing it. Without this recognition, your efforts to make the case that you can solve the problem will be futile. These situations will continue to be leads, not prospects, until the problem is recognized. Also, many individuals resent others telling them that they have problems before they recognize them.

Once the information you obtain indicates that the organization has recognized the problem, focus on determining whether funds are available to hire someone to solve the problem. A good place to start is with the annual budgeting process; this is when organizations determine priorities for funding in the coming fiscal year, including new positions. Focus your research and plug into your network for contacts that may be familiar with the problem or organization to determine if an unadvertised opportunity is under consideration for funding. If the opportunity or position is under consideration for funding, qualify the lead as a prospect.

Once you determine that an organization recognizes the problem and that the position is funded, turn your attention to connecting with the individuals who will make the hiring decision. This may sound simple, but gaining access to the decision maker can be a quite challenge. Some decision makers appreciate individuals approaching them directly to offer their knowledge and expertise to help them solve their problems. Others rely on referrals from trusted friends and colleagues. And, there are the decision makers who rely solely on the traditional hiring process of posting positions, having human resources or a recruiter screen applicants, and then conducting interviews. In these situations, your efforts to connect with the decision maker may be futile. To determine the most effective approach to the decision maker, rely on your network to connect you to individuals who know the preferences of the decision makers and how hiring decisions are made within the organizations you target.

When is the best time to approach a prospect? Factors that influence timing include seasonality, funding process, and status of the company or organization.

There is seasonality in hiring and promotions. To pursue opportunities, the best times to connect with a company are:

- January–early June.
- Between Labor Day and Thanksgiving.

January–early June is an excellent time to approach companies whose fiscal year coincides with the calendar year (January–December) when the availability of funds for hiring is usually at its highest point—and the earlier in the year the better. Business conditions can change as the year progresses. Sales projections may decline due to actions of competitors or adverse economic conditions. Costs may rise higher than assumed when the annual budget was developed. As a consequence, companies may delay or even eliminate new or open positions, promotions, reorganizations, and new projects. Your chances of getting an audience to demonstrate your capabilities are higher if you approach companies before business conditions become less favorable. As a hiring decision maker, I learned to hire and promote as early in the year as the processes would allow, reducing the chances of having my hiring and promotion plans being unfavorably impacted by changes in business conditions.

You should adjust the timing of your approach for companies whose fiscal period does not coincide with the calendar year. For companies with a July–June fiscal year, July–December would correspond to the January–June period in companies whose fiscal years coincide with the calendar year. The fiscal year for public companies is disclosed in annual reports. For private companies, visit the companies' websites or consult with contacts within your network to determine the fiscal year.

Vacations make it difficult to establish interview schedules from mid–June to Labor Day. Your approach to an organization may not get immediate attention during this period. Your capability to solve problems that the organization is encountering could even be *lost in the shuffle* with information that arrives from your competitors during this time. After Labor Day and summer vacations, it is easier for companies to establish interview schedules and decision makers are more available for you to approach them. In companies whose fiscal year coincides with the calendar year, executives and managers also start their final push to accomplish their annual objectives before reaching the Thanksgiving and Christmas holidays. Keep in mind that annual individual performance bonuses and merit pay increases are most likely based on the accomplishment of objectives. The possibility that you could help an executive or manager make the final push to accomplish her or his annual objectives could move the individual to invite you to discuss how you could help.

Managers and executives also push to fill open positions during the latter part of the fiscal year because they do not want to run the risk of losing funding for the positions for the next fiscal year. Senior management may tell managers and executives that the need to fill the position must not have been that urgent if the function or organization operated effectively for several months without the position being filled. Again, use information you gather from annual reports, visits to company websites, and from your network to determine the company's fiscal year.

The funding process reflects the phases of initiatives, programs, and projects that companies follow to execute business strategies. The three basic phases are concept, planning, and execution. Phases also drive hiring and promotions decisions.

Phase	Focus	Hiring, Assignments
Concept	• Identify/assess the problem, opportunity, or need	• Internal, special, or temporary assignments • External consultants or temporary personnel
Planning	• Determine solutions • Establish how project or initiative will be managed • Establish execution plan (tasks, responsibilities, dates, milestones)	• Determine human resource needs • Initiate hiring, promotions, personnel moves (solicit applications, arrange interviews)
Execution	• Implement solution	• Hire, promote, and make personnel moves and organizational changes

To qualify leads based on the phases of initiatives, programs, and projects, questions you should ask yourself, research, or address with your network contacts include:

- In which phase are my strongest skills and capabilities in demand?
- Can I offer *full-cycle* experience (Concept to Execution)?
- Are there opportunities to join companies in a temporary assignment that could evolve into a permanent position?

Skills and capabilities in demand during the concept phase include generating ideas, distinguishing between causes and symptoms, and organizing information into core concepts.

The planning phase would require the ability to transform a concept into a solution, define goals and objectives, establish an approach to implementing the solution, and generating a sequence of actions and tasks to accomplish objectives.

The execution phase would require the ability to manage people and tasks as well as a track record for completing projects and assignments on time and within budget.

In terms of full-cycle experience, you may be that versatile professional with broad experience who could provide continuity for managing or contributing from the concept through execution phases.

When you join an organization in a temporary assignment, you create the opportunity to demonstrate the value you can offer. This demonstration of value could lead to the organization offering a permanent position to you.

As the CEO of your *Business of Me*, you know your product (skills and capabilities) and the situations in which you can excel. You established this when you developed your product and personal brand and reflected this in your personal summary.

The status of a company or an organization can be influenced by reorganizations, divestitures, acquisitions, and resignations of key employees—especially executives. These events create openings. To capitalize on an opportunity created by the resignation of an executive, you can use what I call the *trailing executive tactic*. When executives resign, companies initiate a search to fill the position or promote someone internally to the position, thus creating a need to fill a lower position. You can discover resignations by reviewing trade and industry publications and by checking the "Who's Who" or "People on the Move" section of publications or websites. The trailing executive tactic may position you to strike quickly after a resignation—before the opportunity is known to your competitors. Your action may provide the opportunity for a company to save on a search fee by connecting with the company before it enters into an agreement with a search firm.

Another angle to the trailing executive tactic is focusing on opportunities that are created once a new executive joins a company. For instance, your research and information obtained from your network could reveal that the executive and you share the common experience of solving the problems prevailing in his or her new company. Or, the executive may have a preference for solutions, methods, or techniques of which you are knowledgeable. You and the executive may also be alumni of the same university, have experience in the same industry, or share common network connections. Think about the tendency of individuals to seek familiarity when they move into an unfamiliar environment. You can present yourself as something with which the executive is familiar. Again, I cannot overemphasize the importance of establishing an effective network to migrate the know, like, and trust path to productive relationships.

Approach Prospects

You have prospects! But, you cannot make the sale (get hired or promoted) until you present your product (skills and capabilities) to a decision maker—that is, you must have an interview. A successful approach to prospects is one that results in a *direct discussion* with the decision maker about how your skills and capabilities can satisfy the needs of the prospect. To enhance the probability of success, you should:

- Establish a common connection or point of reference to the prospect.
- Determine how the prospect prefers to be approached.
- Take as much control as possible to move from the connection to "Presenting to the Prospect."

By establishing a common connection or point of reference, you build a foundation of trust upon which the prospect and you can advance to a discussion of the prospect's problem and your ability to solve it. Common connections are individuals with whom the prospect and you are both connected. Points of reference could include links to common organizations or experiences.

Common connections carry more weight than points of reference because of the power of relationships. For example, a prospect can pick up the phone and get an opinion of you from the common connection. In other words, your connections can serve as *trust transfer agents*. Tap into your network to identify common connections. (Here we go again with networking.) You can identify common connections with decision makers by exploring:

- Memberships in common organizations and network groups (traditional and Internet-based)
- Employment at the same company, especially in the same function (sales, marketing, finance, information technology, et al.)
- Alumni directories of universities

In addition, connections to individuals at higher rather than lower levels will be more helpful to you. First, an executive with whom you are meeting is more likely to know someone who is on an equal professional playing field. Second, connections who can offer a product similar to yours might view you as a competitor; instead of helping you, they may actually hinder your attempt to make a connection. Finally, decision makers do not usually look to subordinates or persons lower in the organization for referrals. Since there are exceptions to every rule, use every opportunity to network and build strong, trusting relationships. (I once landed an interview with an executive based on the friendship between his wife and the wife of an individual who used to work for me. The wives had been friends since childhood. The interview eventually led to a job offer.)

You can identify common points of reference by seeking:

- Articles the prospect has written
- Comments the prospect has made about a trend, issue, opportunity, problem, or development
- Articles addressing trends, issues, opportunities, problems, or developments in which your connection may be interested (use reputable sources)

You have identified the common connection or point of reference. Now, what is the best way to approach the prospect? Individuals have personal preferences as to how they are approached. Following are considerations for determining how you should approach a prospect:

- Does the prospect prefer to be contacted initially by e-mail or telephone?
- Does the prospect's administrative assistant screen all phone calls or review all correspondence addressed to the prospect?
- What time of the day does the prospect allocate to reading correspondence or receiving telephone calls?

- How does the time of day, week, or month factor into the willingness of the prospect to receive correspondence or a call from you?
- Does the prospect like to *get to the point immediately* or prefer to have a *get comfortable* exchange before getting to the point of the discussion?

You can consult with individuals in your network for information on how the prospect prefers to be approached. Following are additional considerations:

- If you cannot determine the preference for e-mail or telephone, make the initial contact by e-mail. Individuals can read e-messages whenever it is convenient for them, allowing them a bit more flexibility—using a personal device (e.g. Blackberry) if they are traveling on business, or are at home, or even during a conference call (executives are required to multitask). Individuals will seldom respond favorably to what they perceive as an infringement or uninvited demand on their time. Think of how you feel when you get an unsolicited phone call.
- The delivery and confirmation of receipt of e-mails are instant.
- If you find that your prospect's administrative assistant screens all correspondence:

  o Get the administrative assistant's name and telephone number
  o Call to verify the assistant's e-mail address
  o Inform the assistant that you will be sending correspondence and ask if he or she will forward it the prospect

The impression you make on an administrative assistant can enhance or inhibit your ability to connect with a prospect. Many executives and managers spend more time with their administrative assistants than anyone else. Executives frequently have had the same assistant as they climbed the organizational ladder. They rely on their assistant's opinions; remember to be polite and respectful when you interact with an assistant. Recognize his or her importance; remember his or her name and thank the assistant for helping you.

The time of month can also be an important factor for connecting with a prospect in the financial area. Individuals engaged in financial reporting are busy during the first five-to-seven work days following the end of a month or fiscal period. Individuals in the financial area are also busy during the first three weeks following the end of a fiscal quarter as they are engaged in preparing information for release to the public. Executives may be in discussions with the investment community concerning the company's quarterly results and financial position. There is a chance that correspondence will be ignored or lost in the shuffle if received during busy periods, and phone calls may be annoying.

Be mindful that the purpose of the approach is to get the prospect or decision maker to agree to a direct discussion with you, preferably face-to-face. (This is the transition to the next step in the selling process, "Present to the Prospect.") You must take control. Ask for the discussion. If you don't ask for a discussion, don't be surprised if you don't get one. When you do not ask, you leave it to the decision maker to determine what you want. More importantly, not asking may indicate that you do not take initiative.

Components of an effective e-mail approach include:

1. Attention Getter: Opening statement connecting the prospect and you to a common connection.
2. Bait: Brief statement of the types of challenges your prospect may be encountering. (You may have something to offer.)
3. Brief statement of your brand and your success addressing the challenges (skills and capabilities).
4. Three of your accomplishments that support your capability to address the challenges (evidence of your skills and capabilities).
5. Call to action. (What do you want to happen as a result of the approach—the next step?)
6. How the prospect can contact you.
7. Expression of your appreciation for reading your message.

Following is an example of an effective e-mail message to a prospect. It is from an information technology professional to the chief information officer (CIO) of a company. The common connection is a former colleague of the CIO who has remained friends with the CIO since going their separate ways in the business world. The professional has the approval of the common connection to use his name, and has learned from research that the CIO's current company has decided to implement a global Enterprise Resource Planning solution (ERP) called SAP.

Mr. Williams:

John Butler suggested I contact you; he believes that a discussion with you might be beneficial.

I have read that your company has decided to implement SAP. As a supporter and user of SAP, I can attest to the benefits that it can deliver to an enterprise. Having successfully managed components of a global SAP solution, I am aware of the challenges SAP presents to ensuring the availability, reliability, and efficiency of information systems infrastructure operations. I have established a reputation as a leader and problem solver by unraveling complex information systems infrastructure problems, delivering projects on time and within budget, and building strong relationships between information technology and trade partners and internal business partners. I have:

- Increased systems availability from 96% to 99.9% by leading the selection and implementation of systems management tools to support an SAP environment.
- Reduced supply chain systems service disruptions by 80% within six months by leading the integration of systems management solutions between the company and its leading trade partners.
- Strengthened partnership between the information technology organization and the end-user community by introducing customer quality review boards that increased the participation of end users in the development of value-based service level agreements.

I would like to learn more about the opportunities and challenges your organization is facing. I will call your office the week of March 3 to schedule a discussion. If you would like to contact me before then, you can reach me at (200) 555-1000 or by e-mail at cathsmith03@email.net.

Mr. Williams, thank you for your consideration. I look forward to meeting you.

Catherine Smith

Present to Prospects

The interview provides the *stage* for you to present the benefits of your product to decision makers. There are many kinds of interviews, including screening, behavioral, group, stress, and informational. In the end, however, interviews focus on determining if the prospect or the company should:

- Spend the time and effort to consider you for employment
- Proceed with extending an offer of employment to you

Abundant information on successful interviewing is available in books, periodicals, and on the Internet. This information includes:

- Preparing for interviews
- Frequently asked or challenging questions
- Dressing and grooming
- Interviewing etiquette

This information will be helpful in turning a prospect into a customer—or, in your case, your new employer. As you read the information available from these sources, I suggest that you keep in mind the following points that can increase your chances for a successful interview:

- Work is a problem to be solved. If you convince the prospect that you have the skills and capabilities to solve the problem, the prospect will hire you.
- Seek to understand the needs of the prospect. The agreement of the prospect to meet with you indicates that the intelligence you gathered on the company's needs *may be* accurate. Ask questions during the interview to *confirm* the accuracy of your intelligence.

- The questions you ask are just as important, possibly more important, as the statements you make. Pose thoughtful and concise questions that reflect your interest in satisfying the needs of the prospect and the company. Keep in mind that *it takes an intelligent person to ask an intelligent question.*
- *Dance* with the interviewer. The interviewer is your potential customer. The potential customer wants to focus the interview on satisfying his or her needs. *Let the interviewer lead the dance.* Respond with questions and answers that demonstrate your ability to satisfy the needs.
- Determine whether the interview is a *how* or *who* interview. *How* interviews focus primarily on whether you have the skills and capabilities to satisfy the prospect's needs. *Who* interviews focus on your ability to fit into the organization. Fitting into an organization addresses your chemistry versus the chemistry or culture of the organization. In how interviews, interviewers tend to probe the information in your résumé. In who interviews, interviewers ask questions related to your management or work style, your approach to getting things done, and even personal information, such as your interests. Again, remember to dance with the interviewer so that you can recognize if the interview is a how or who interview.

Always send a follow-up e-mail to the decision maker and other members of the interview team within two days after the interview. Little touches, like sending a separate e-mail to each interviewer and personalizing each one (i.e., including a comment about a common contact or experience) really goes a long way and will help you stand out from your competitors. An effective follow-up communication will:

1. Reinforce your capability to satisfy the needs of the prospect.
2. Provide information that the interviewers requested, but you were unable to provide during the interview.
3. Strengthen the relationships you initiated with the decision maker and other members of the interview team.

Following is an example of an effective follow-up communication.

Mr. Williams:

Thank you for the opportunity to discuss the global SAP implementation that you will initiate in the third quarter. I believe that I could make a significant contribution to a successful implementation. The challenges you are facing are similar to those that I addressed when I managed the infrastructure component of the global SAP implementation at Global Products Manufacturing Corporation.

Attached is the Project Interaction Diagram (PID) that we discussed. It is the model I used to clarify the roles and responsibilities of the project team that I led.

I enjoyed our discussion of ITIL, and I agree that it is a significant tool for managing information services.

Please contact me at (200) 555-1000 or by e-mail at cathsmith03@email.net if you need additional information.

I look forward to continuing our discussion of your needs and challenges and the contributions I could make.

Catherine Smith

Overcome Rejection

You researched the situation and gathered intelligence on the needs of the prospect. You presented your product and related its capabilities to the needs of the prospect, but the prospect did not purchase your product. Rejection is a part of running a business—in your case, your *Business of Me*. All prospects will not purchase, but that does not mean you have failed. Factors that keep prospects from becoming customers may have been beyond your control. This could include:

- Timing
- Status of the organization or decision maker
- Chemistry

A change in business conditions, restructuring, or a reorganization may have caused your prospect to delay filling the position or may have resulted in eliminating the opening altogether. Also, the company's needs may have changed, and they no longer match your skills and capabilities. The company may have changed the scope of responsibilities, so the position for which you interviewed may have changed, forcing you out of the ring of contenders because your skills and capabilities are no longer what they need.

Sometimes, the company hasn't experienced a change, but the decision maker may have decided to leave the company, been promoted, or changed responsibilities. The decision maker's successor may have altered the approach to satisfying the company's needs.

An offer might not have been extended to you because your interview may have revealed that the culture of the organization and your personality were not a good fit. The conflict could have been between the decision maker or one of the other members of the interview team and you. There also could have been competition between one of the members of the interview team and you that you did not realize during the interview.

I experienced this once when I interviewed for a position. I was convinced that the company was going to make an offer to me, especially since the interview with the person to whom I would report had gone well. Our discussion hit on all cylinders in terms of what was needed versus what I offered and his management style versus my work style. It was the same with all but one of the members of the interview team. On leaving, I felt the result of the interview with that individual was a draw. It was not a knockout, but it was not a cause for alarm. I was surprised when I was informed that the company would not extend an offer to me. I then had some doubts about how well I had interviewed and whether I needed to change my ways. Subsequently, I learned from a college classmate who worked in the organization that the interview that I thought was a draw was not a draw. The individual believed that I would be a formidable competitor for his advancement to leader of the organization. As the CEO of the *Business of Him*, he was not going to create competition.

In future interviews, I paid close attention to the relationships I could have with members of the interview team. I positioned myself as someone who could contribute to the success of the organization rather than as a competitor to members of the team. (Hire me and we all will win.)

Instead of looking at rejection as a failure, look at is as a learning experience that can help you improve how you sell your product. After receiving a rejection, ask the decision maker or someone with whom you established an excellent rapport to provide feedback on your interview performance. This information can help you improve the selling of your product to prospects in the future.

Whether or not you obtain feedback, always respond to a rejection. Express your appreciation for the opportunity to interview and your willingness to discuss how you could satisfy the needs of the company in the future. This keeps the door open for you and sets the stage for a future interview if another position opens or if business conditions improve. Following up can also strengthen your connection to the decision maker or other members of the interview team. For example, one of your interviewers might move to a different company where there is a chance you will be remembered, and he or she might contact you for an open position with needs that fit well with your product. You may also be referred to other opportunities, especially inquiries from search firms or peers who may need your product. They may even become members of your network!

Close

You are feeling great. You presented your product. You received strong indications that the prospect will purchase (hire you). However, remember that there is no sale until the prospect makes an offer to purchase (extends a job offer) and you accept the offer. Before receiving the offer, list considerations that are important to you. Doing this in advance will avoid the chance of the offer driving what you *think* you want versus letting what you want drive your evaluation of the offer. Following are things you should consider.

- Compensation
- Timing of your initial performance review
- Vacation and other benefits
- Reporting date
- Allowances to attend professional conferences to continue your personal development
- Criteria essential to your success, such as your role in selecting or changing members of your team

Get what you want *before* you accept the offer. Your negotiating power diminishes significantly after you accept the offer.

Follow-up

You received the offer and it meets your requirements. You may receive an employment contract to sign. The contract may include the starting salary and confirmation of the items you negotiated. If for some reason you do not receive an employment contract, keep a copy of the offer letter and send an e-mail confirming your acceptance of the offer. This will be a reference that you can use if issues related to the terms of your employment evolve, especially if the person who hired you moves to another position or leaves the company.

Summary: What, When, How

Structure

1. Identify leads
2. Qualify leads to determine prospects
3. Approach prospects
4. Present to prospects
5. Overcome rejection
6. Close
7. Follow up

Filing Cabinet

Situation/Need	Information on File
Planning job search, career campaign	<ul><li>Selling Process<ul><li>o Identify leads</li><li>o Qualify leads</li><li>o Approach prospects</li><li>o Overcome rejection</li></ul></li><li>Target Position Description</li><li>Personal Summary</li><li>Channels to prioritize efforts</li><li>Managing relationships with search firms</li></ul>
Interviewing	<ul><li>Present to prospects (Step 4, Selling Process)</li><li>Career Summary and Career Highlights components of your Personal Summary</li></ul>
Negotiating job offers	<ul><li>Close (Step 6, Selling Process)</li><li>Follow-up (Step 7, Selling Process)</li></ul>
Building personal network	<ul><li>Know, Like, Trust path to establishing relationships</li><li>Personal Summary</li><li>Overcome rejection (Step 5, Selling Process)</li></ul>
Executing career plan	<ul><li>Overcome rejection (Step 5, Selling Process)</li></ul>

Sale Made = Value Received

Work is a problem to be solved. You are hired when you persuade the decision maker that you can solve the problem.

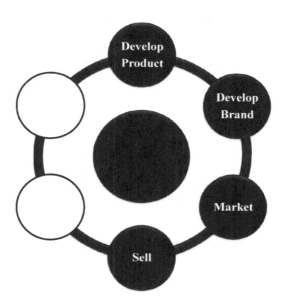

Section III

Prove Your Value
Deliver: Provide What You Promise

Chapter 5:

Deliver: Provide What You Promise

"It is an immutable law in business that words are words, explanations are explanations, promises are promises, but only performance is reality."
—Harold Geneen, former CEO of ITT, who led the growth of ITT from $760 million to $17 billion

Do I do what I say I can do?

Deliver: Business Management Process

Think of a commercial depicting a person enjoying a drive in her automobile as it navigates smoothly through the countryside and city traffic, quickly responding to the driver's demands. This advertising will encourage customers seeking that kind of driving experience to purchase the automobile. If the automobile performs according to the expectations created by the advertisement, customers will repeat their purchase and encourage others to purchase the automobile. If, however, the performance of the automobile does not meet the expectations, customers will be disappointed, electing not to purchase automobiles from the manufacturer again—and not encouraging others to purchase.

Companies develop products to satisfy the needs of their target markets. They brand their products and set expectations for customers by communicating the benefits customers will experience if they purchase their products. The success of a company depends on its ability to meet the expectations of its customers.

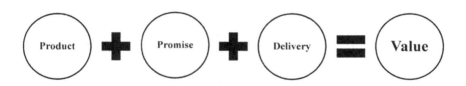

Companies set market share and customer satisfaction objectives to define their success in meeting the expectations of customers. They use tools such as customer satisfaction surveys and market share reports to measure success. Companies also develop contingency plans to respond to changes in the marketplace such as the introduction of new products and product improvements by competitors.

Deliver: *The Business of Me*

Just like companies, your success depends on whether your performance meets the expectations of your customers—the individuals who evaluate your performance or who can influence your performance evaluations. In fact, you should strive to exceed expectations to beat your competition—others who are seeking the same positions and compensation you are seeking. Your product development, personal branding, marketing, and selling will be negated if you do not deliver on your brand promise.

By reading this chapter, you will:

1. Be introduced to a process for managing your performance to meet or exceed the expectations of the individuals who evaluate your performance.
2. Become familiar with measures you can take to maximize your control of the performance evaluations you receive.
3. Get ideas on how you can increase your chances of receiving exceptional performance evaluations.
4. Become familiar with actions you can take to manage situations that could have a negative impact on your performance evaluations.
5. Get ideas on how to leverage the management of your performance to enhance your career advancement opportunities.

Following are steps that you can utilize to apply the principles of the deliver component of the Business Management Process to the management of your performance.

1. Set the performance stage that will provide a high probability of success for you.
2. Ensure that your manager and you have a common understanding of what is expected of you.
3. Create the appraisal that you want to receive at the end of the appraisal period.

4. Establish a *personal performance monitoring system.*
5. Establish contingencies if circumstances that impact your performance change.

Set the Stage

By operating your *Business of Me,* you establish your personal brand. Your brand captures the value you can offer. You communicate this value when you market and sell your capabilities and skills (your product). This communication is your brand promise.

You also know that there are factors over which you have direct control and factors that are beyond your direct control. By focusing on your brand promise and the factors that you can control, you can design your performance stage—the platform that enables you to play to your strengths. Your performance stage will provide leverage for you as you seek to reach agreement on performance goals and evaluation criteria with your performance evaluators, thus increasing your chances of receiving exceptional performance evaluations. Following are questions you should answer to establish your performance stage:

1. What needs to be done by others to ensure that you can achieve your objectives?
2. Have those individuals, teams, or departments committed to accomplishing what is expected of them?
3. How does the time allowed for achieving your potential performance objectives compare to the time that it took to achieve similar objectives?
4. How does the funding compare to funding for similar assignments?
5. Are the required funds and resources available? If not, when will funds and resources be approved?

I recommend that you address the first two questions to individuals who will evaluate your performance and/or the persons upon whom you will depend to achieve your performance objectives. Note that I do not limit addressing your questions to your manager or supervisor because there may be instances where you may be assigned to a project team or initiative and your performance evaluation will be determined by input from the leaders or your peers on the teams responsible for achieving the objectives of the projects and initiatives.

Sources of information for answering questions 3–5 are captured in the following chart.

Information Needed	Source
• How long did it take to accomplish the objectives? • How much funding did it require? • How many resources were assigned (number of people)?	Final reports for similar projects and initiatives
Are there red flags (warning signals) related to the assignment I am considering?	Audits of terminated projects and initiatives that were not successful
When will funding be approved and resources assigned?	• Individuals who have been engaged in the concept and/or planning phases of the project or initiative • Project Management Office in the Information Technology Group in your company (Many company programs and initiatives have an information technology component. Project management offices are responsible for tracking the approval of funding of projects and initiatives.) • Individuals engaged in the development of long-range financial plans for your organization or company

"Promise only what you can deliver. Then deliver more than you promise."
—Author unknown

Ensure Common Understanding of Expectations

You have set the performance stage. Now, you must ensure that your performance evaluator and you are *singing from the same hymnbook*. Do not assume that the persons who will evaluate your performance have the same understanding as you as to what you are expected to deliver or achieve. Two people can look at the same information and come to different conclusions. During my corporate career, I witnessed disputes between managers and subordinates concerning performance ratings. Many of the disputes were due to misunderstandings between the manager and the subordinate concerning expectations. We may *think* that we have agreement with someone else, but we only *know* that we have agreement when both parties say the same thing and put it in writing. Following are five essential questions for which you and your manager must have the same answer to ensure that you have a common understanding of what is expected of you:

1. When will we know that the objectives have been achieved or the assignment completed?
2. When will I no longer have to work on this assignment?
3. What do I have to do or provide to bring this assignment to a successful close?
4. What resources and funds will be provided to support the accomplishment of my objectives?
5. What criteria will be used to rate my performance in terms of meeting or exceeding expectations?

An example of the importance of setting common expectations is the success that the Green Bay Packers experienced when Vince Lombardi coached the team. Vince Lombardi accepted the offer to become the head coach of the Green Bay Packers professional football team for the 1959 season. The Packers had become a lackluster team in recent years, finishing among the lowest performing teams in the National Football League (NFL). When Lombardi arrived in Green Bay, he created a *picture* or vision for the Packers players of how it would look and feel to be champions. That vision, *seeing* what was desired, became the expectations that became the standard for being a Green Bay Packer. Green Bay Packers players performed to these expectations and became the best team in the NFL during the 1960s, winning five NFL championships during Lombardi's nine-year tenure as the team's head coach. Just like the Green Bay Packers during the Lombardi era, your chances of success increase significantly when the evaluator of your performance and you have common expectations of your performance.

Create the Appraisal You Want

Jack Canfield, the co-author of the *Chicken Soup for the Soul* series of books and a renowned success coach, relates the power of creating a personal vision of what a person wants to achieve. Jack and his partner set a goal of selling more than one million copies of their first book. They used white out to place the name of their book on the list of best selling books in an edition of the *New York Times*. Referring to their "*New York Times* Best Selling Books List" was a source of inspiration and motivation as they overcame many challenges marketing their book. More than one million copies of the book were sold within eighteen months of the book's release.

You can clarify your personal vision of what you want to achieve by creating a vision, before the appraisal period starts, of the performance appraisal that you want to receive at the end of the appraisal period. To make your desired performance appraisal feel real or authentic:

- Use the same form that your company will use to prepare your actual appraisal
- Include the performance objectives upon which you and your manager agreed
- Use the same criteria upon which your manager and you agreed to evaluate your performance
- Sign your manager's name and your name on the appraisal form
- Place your desired appraisal on the wall of your office or cubicle or place it in a folder to carry with you every day

Having a clear picture of what you want to achieve will also help you guard against *scope creeps*. Scope creeps are requests from individuals and events that can cause you to lose focus on achieving what is expected of you. It makes you think before taking on the, "*Oh, by the way*" requests.

Personal Performance Monitoring System

A *personal performance monitoring system* warns you that something could be going wrong. It functions like a thermometer. You may feel fine, but a body temperature of 100 degrees tells you that everything is not quite right. Your performance monitoring system could include:

- Personal leading indicators
- Monthly or quarterly status reports written to yourself
- Quarterly reviews with a peer, mentor, or your coach to get an objective view of how well you are performing

Personal leading indicators could include the actual versus the assumed timing of the approval of funds and assignment of resources; commitments of individuals, teams, or departments upon which your performance is dependent; and key accomplishments or milestones. For example, your manager and you agreed that an assignment to be completed by September 30 would have funding approved by March 31. Based on the agreement, you established the timing of funding as a leading indicator. Funding is actually approved in July, thus making the accomplishment of your performance objective improbable. By establishing the approval of the funding leading indicator, you can initiate timely actions to make the changes needed to adjust the terms of your performance evaluation.

Establish Contingencies

Establishing your personal performance monitoring system points you to realizing that circumstances can change and situations can develop that could inhibit your ability to achieve your performance objectives. That is why it is important that you establish contingency plans and define adjustments you could make ahead of time. Following are steps for establishing an effective contingency plan:

1. List changes and developments that could impact your ability to achieve your objectives.
2. Determine alternative actions that you could take to offset or minimize the impact.
3. Evaluate the advantages and disadvantages of the alternative actions.
4. Establish your contingency plan based on your evaluation of advantages and disadvantages.

5. Use the following format to present your recommendations to your manager or the person who will evaluate your performance.

    a. Situation: What changes or developments could inhibit your ability to achieve your performance objectives?

    b. Impact: What is the impact of the changes or developments on your ability to achieve your objectives?

    c. Recommendations: What actions do you recommend and what impact will these actions have on the achievement of your objectives?

When you establish a contingency plan, you:

- Can focus your manager's attention on factors that you can control while identifying factors that are beyond your control and need to be addressed by someone who can control these factors.
- Realize the benefit of being the *person with the plan*. (Have you noticed that in times of uncertainty, individuals listen to the person with a plan for dealing with the situation, and that person has a great deal of influence on deciding what actions will be taken?)
- Demonstrate that you can think ahead and take the initiative—leadership traits that will help you during the current appraisal period as well as strengthen consideration of you for higher visibility assignments and positions with greater responsibilities.

Summary: What, When, How

Structure

1. Set the performance stage that will provide a high probability of success for you.
2. Ensure that your manager and you have a common understanding of what is expected of you.
3. Create the appraisal that you want to receive at the end of the appraisal period.
4. Establish a personal performance monitoring system.
5. Establish contingencies if circumstances that impact your performance change.

Filing Cabinet

Situation/Need	Information on File
Deciding what assignments you will pursue	• Career Development Plan • Positioning and Passion components of the 6Ps of Marketing
Establishing your annual performance objectives and evaluation criteria with your manager	• Appraisal you want to receive • Reports on results of similar projects and assignments • Discussions with individuals assigned to IT Project Management Office • Discussions with individuals engaged in long-range planning
Negotiating adjustments to your performance evaluation criteria	• Personal Performance Monitoring System • Contingency plans

"An acre of performance is worth a whole world of promise."
—William Dean Howells, author of *Christmas Every Day*

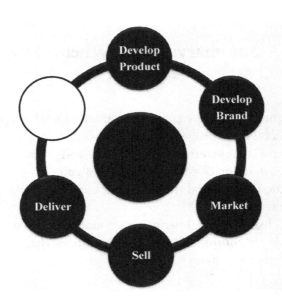

Section IV

Learn and Adjust

**Continuous
Improvement**

Chapter 6:

Learn and Adjust: Keep Up with Change

"The one unchangeable certainty is that nothing is certain or unchangeable."
—John F. Kennedy

Am I managing change or is change managing me?

Learn & Adjust: Business Management Process

Lotus 1–2–3 was a very successful product when it was introduced in the 1980s. It increased productivity by automating the preparation and maintenance of spreadsheets, a core activity for preparing and presenting quantitative information in the business world. It replaced the thirteen-column worksheet pads and the calculator. Being proficient in the use of Lotus 1–2–3 became a core skill for business professionals. Lotus Corporation was sitting on top of the office software applications world. The company introduced improvements to the software, but offered no significant breakthroughs.

Then, Microsoft introduced Excel with features and capabilities beyond what 1–2–3 offered. Microsoft not only introduced enhancements to the preparation and maintenance of spreadsheets, it also integrated the preparation and use of spreadsheets into other activities such as presentations, reports, and other documents. As a result, Excel became the number one and dominant spreadsheet application. Lotus 1–2–3 eventually faded from the scene.

The needs of customers change and competitors will seek to satisfy those needs by introducing products with additional features, capabilities, and functionality. Successful businesses understand that they must continue to meet the expectations of their customers by:

- Sustaining the performance of their current products
- Refreshing and upgrading their product offerings

These actions are requirements for continued success—not options.

Learn and Adjust: *The Business of Me*

Sustaining your performance and refreshing and upgrading your product (your skills and capabilities) are also requirements for the continued success of your *Business of Me*—not options. You may have developed skills and capabilities based on the needs of the employment marketplace in the past and delivered on your brand promise, resulting in increases in your compensation, promotions, and new career opportunities. Then, you hit a plateau. The raises become less frequent and smaller and the promotions stop. You are no longer assigned to high-visibility projects. New career opportunities seem to be beyond your reach.

You may have ridden or sat on your laurels because you did not recognize and respond to changes in the employment marketplace such as the emergence of new business concepts, business models, and problem-solving and analytical techniques. These developments changed the needs of the employment marketplace and what companies would pay for certain skills and capabilities. By not responding to the developments, you allowed the changes to diminish your competitive position.

By reading this chapter you will:

1. Be introduced to measures you can take to maintain or strengthen your competitive position for promotions and new career opportunities.
2. Be familiar with resources you can utilize to stay abreast of opportunities emerging in the employment marketplace.
3. Get ideas on how you can position yourself to grow your compensation.

Let's address how you can sustain your performance and refresh and upgrade your product—your skills and capabilities.

Sustaining Your Performance

We covered actions that you can take to deliver performance that meets or exceeds expectations in chapter five, "Deliver." The value implications of continuing this level of performance are captured in a method that many companies use to differentiate performance and the granting of annual merit pay increases to individual employees. This method entails the use of a normalized distribution or bell-shaped curve. Performance ratings are given to each employee to create the bell-shaped distribution of ratings for all employees.

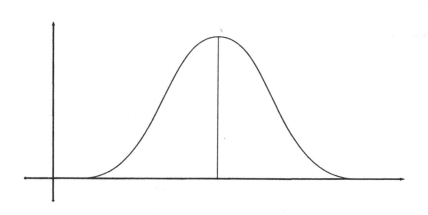

Employees with ratings on the left side of the curve are higher than the overall population average, while individual ratings on the right side are lower than the average. Let's use an example of how the performance ratings that an individual employee receives impact the value that an employee realizes over a period of five years. The salaries in the table below are based on an initial annual salary of $75,000 for the individual. Future potential salaries for the individual reflect the difference in annual merit pay increases that the individual could receive based on the position of her or his performance rating in the distribution of performance ratings for all employees in the organization.

Annual Salary Increase	1%	2%	3%	4%	5%
Year 1	75,750	76,500	77,250	78,000	78,750
Year 2	76,508	78,030	79,568	81,120	82,688
Year 3	77,273	79,591	81,955	84,365	86,822
Year 4	78,045	81,182	84,413	87,739	91,163
Year 5	78,826	82,806	86,946	91,249	95,721

Receiving a 5 percent versus 1 percent annual merit increase will result in $16,895 of higher compensation in Year 5. Receiving a 5 percent versus 2 percent annual merit increase will result in $12,915 of higher compensation in Year 5. Utilizing the personal performance management process covered in chapter five, "Deliver," will help you manage the factors related to your performance that you can control to sustain your performance and position you to grow your compensation.

Refreshing and Upgrading Your Product

The business process for refreshing and upgrading product offerings is often designated as the *Continuous Improvement Process*. Through continuous improvement, companies keep their products competitive and thus grow the value they generate for their investors. Companies enable the Continuous Improvement Process by:

- Soliciting and acting on feedback from customers
- Researching and incorporating marketplace trends and developments into their products
- Monitoring and quickly responding to the actions of competitors
- Soliciting advice from advisors, especially their board of directors

Executing your *Personal Continuous Improvement Process* will enable you to maintain and even strengthen your competitive position in the employment marketplace and grow the value you create for yourself. Listed below are ten actions you can take to enable your personal improvement process:

- Participate in 360-degree feedback surveys and act on the feedback you receive
- Get a mentor
- Hire a coach
- Designate a specific and recurring time to research new business models, tools, and techniques
- Join a professional organization in your field
- Keep your *fingers* in the marketplace
- Research current curriculum in your field at colleges and universities
- Connect with and observe new employees, including recent college graduates, who join your company
- Take an *investment approach* to managing your career
- Establish your personal board of directors

Participation in 360-degree surveys was addressed in the "Persona" section of chapter three, "Marketing." The feedback you receive may indicate that you need to refresh or upgrade your skills or improve your delivery (the way you perform) or your management of relationships with others. The feedback may also reveal the need to change the way you present yourself. (We covered this in the "Presentation" section of chapter three.)

Mentors, especially members of senior management at your company, can alert you to developments and opportunities on which you can capitalize to give you an edge over your competitors.

Coaches differ from mentors in that mentors provide advice, perspective, and models for your personal development while coaching is built on the cornerstones of awareness and responsibility. Coaches help you become aware of your capabilities and needs and serve as your partner by ensuring that you hold yourself accountable for executing your improvement process. Coaching arrangements can include individual and group sessions. Individual sessions focus on your specific needs, whereas group sessions involve individuals with similar professional profiles and needs. Also, many coaching organizations, including *Fields of Success,* offer teleseminars, webinars, and workshops that will help you address your improvement needs. You can participate in many of these sessions from home (online) and at times that are convenient for you (e.g. evenings, weekends).

John Maxwell, the well-known author and speaker, said, "Your actions are your priorities." Reserve time on your schedule to read books and articles and search the Internet for trends and developments in your field.

For instance, you could designate Wednesday evening as *professional research night,* or a block of time before your peers, subordinates, and boss arrive at the office. Decide what works best for you and make it a habit. This is the R component (Research) of Research and Development for operating your *Business of Me.*

Professional organizations are exceptional venues for discovering new developments and trends in your field. Some organizations will have their members make presentations while others will have guest speakers who are experts in new developments, trends, and techniques. Do not overlook opportunities presented by joining Internet-based groups; they are diverse and include many people from all regions of the world with different backgrounds and broad experience, ranging from entry level all the way up to executive. You can also survey members to determine new developments and trends that are emerging at their companies and use that information to identify changes and adjustments you need to make to your personal development plans.

Keeping your fingers in the marketplace could include:

- Periodically reviewing job postings at career websites to identify new skills and capabilities the marketplace is demanding and the premium the market is offering (additional compensation).
- Interviewing for positions to get a firsthand view of what the market is demanding.
- Maintaining relationships with search firm consultants to stay abreast of skills and capabilities employers are seeking.
- Establishing relationships with individuals who are unemployed or are in transition. These individuals can be excellent sources of marketplace intelligence because they are deeply immersed in the employment market.
- Participating in conferences sponsored by your company's vendors to become familiar with new techniques, concepts, business models, applications suites, and tools.

Colleges and universities revise and update their curricula to ensure the marketability of their graduates for employment. Review the current curriculums for top-ranked schools to identify courses you can take to stay competitive in your field in the employment marketplace. Your company might pay for the courses you take.

Experienced professionals often overlook the information that new hires can provide on new concepts and techniques that colleges and universities are teaching to their students. Build relationships with new hires from undergraduate and graduate programs by assisting them with their assimilation into your company. You can learn about the latest techniques and concepts by leveraging the relationships you establish with the new hires.

Individuals joining your company from other companies may bring knowledge that could be helpful to you, especially those from firms noted as leaders in your field. Individuals tend to be more open to approaches from other employees when they first join a company because they are looking to learn about the company and establish relationships. You can leverage your knowledge about your company and its culture to gain insight into techniques and tools that are already in use at the new employee's former company.

By investing in upgrading or refreshing your product, you can increase the value you create. I once had a discussion with an information technology professional who was disappointed because his company would not provide the funds he needed to be certified as a Project Management Professional (PMP). The cost of the training was $1,000. I suggested that he research information technology positions at career websites to determine what the market would pay for PMP certification. His research revealed that such positions offered as much as $3,000 in higher compensation versus similar positions that did not require the certification. He and I chuckled at the results of his research. Without applying an *investment mindset* to his product, he would have overlooked an opportunity to generate an annual stream of $3,000 in additional compensation from an investment of $1,000! Your career is an asset. Just like companies, you should seek opportunities that will provide returns on your investments.

Establishing a personal board of directors can also enable your *Personal Continuous Improvement Process.* Let's start with the role that boards serve in the Business Management Process. Companies establish boards to help them address challenges and issues that may impact their ability to create value. Boards are comprised of individuals who bring expertise and diverse perspectives and experience. Boards can help companies focus on things that they may overlook or of which they have limited knowledge.

You will encounter challenges and issues as you manage your *Business of Me.* If the most successful companies in the world endowed with brilliant minds have boards of directors, why can't you? You may be overlooking or have limited knowledge of possibilities, opportunities, and options to improve your position in the employment marketplace to increase the value you can create for yourself.

Recognizing the need for a personal board of directors, how can you establish one? Following are steps you can take to establish your personal board of directors:

1. Identify the challenges and issues you need to address.
2. Prioritize the challenges and issues.
3. Define the type of assistance you need.
4. Establish profiles for potential board members.
5. Recruit your board members.

Sources of information for identifying challenges and issues you need to address include:

- Performance evaluations.
- Feedback from 360-degree and other surveys focused on how you are perceived by your peers, superiors, and subordinates.
- Gaps between your desired and current states in your Professional Development Plan. (Refer to "Developing Your Product" step in the "Product Development: *The Business of Me*" section in chapter one.)
- Information gathered from *keeping your fingers in the marketplace.*
- Discussions with new employees who joined your company from companies known for their leadership in your field.

You may identify several challenges and issues you need to address. However, your time and other resources are limited. How can you prioritize your challenges and issues? How can you determine which challenges are most *important*? Which ones are the most *urgent*? (Which ones should you address first, second, or third?) Following are measures that you can take to determine importance:

- Assign higher levels of importance to qualifications designated as required (versus preferred) in your Target Position Description.

- Consult with someone who has accomplished what you want to achieve to understand which factors had the most significant impact on their success. Apply what you discover to your situation.
- Review your performance appraisals and results from 360-degree feedback surveys and consider observations from your peers, supervisors, and subordinates to pinpoint areas where you need the most improvement.

You can assign urgency to each challenge or issue by asking, "What will be the consequences if I do not address this challenge or issue within the next sixty or ninety days or within a year?"

You can use the following template to apply importance and urgency to prioritize your efforts to address your challenges and issues.

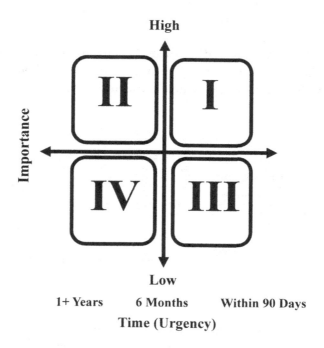

The four quadrants reflect the balancing of importance versus urgency. Assign each challenge to a specific quadrant based on the importance and urgency of the challenge relative to other challenges.

Quadrant	Importance	Time (Urgency)
I	High	Immediate
II	High	Medium to Low
III	Medium to Low	High
IV	Low	Low

You should prioritize your efforts as follows:

- #1: Quadrant I
- #2: Quadrant II
- #3: Quadrant III
- #4: Quadrant IV

Defining the assistance you need focuses on determining the most effective way for you to receive assistance. The effectiveness of that assistance will vary according to the challenges you face and the results of actions you have already taken to address them. In some instances, you may need reinforcement. In other instances, you may need ideas. Following is an example of documenting the match between the types of assistance and challenges.

Challenges	Reinforce	Encourage	Ideas	Perspective
Making presentations that engage my audiences	X			
Getting approval of my ideas and proposals			X	
Establishing and managing relationships with individuals who can influence decisions to hire or promote me				X
Executing my professional development plan		X		

Seeking input from individuals who observe you in the workplace and comments from your performance evaluations and 360-degree survey results can help you match your challenges to the type of assistance you need.

When you define the assistance you need, you get an idea of what to look for in your potential board members. You can capture this information by developing profiles of the individuals you will approach to be members of your personal board of directors. Following are considerations for developing profiles:

- Experience
- Strengths
- Style
- Gender
- Ethnicity

Dimensions of experience include *depth* and *breadth*. Depth of experience may be important when you are seeking to move into a function, discipline, or area in which you have little or no experience to upgrade your product. For instance, an information technology professional with a great deal of experience managing back-end functions such as networks and computer operations may have minimal experience getting approval for his or her ideas and proposals. If the professional's target position requires this experience, a board member who has a distinguished track record for successfully selling ideas to senior management would be an excellent board candidate.

Breadth of experience in a board member is important when you need to look beyond your current environment. For example, you may find that your company adapts new techniques and concepts in your discipline rather than being innovators. You may have witnessed situations in which your company hired individuals from those innovative companies rather than training or developing individuals from within. A board member who works for a company that is an innovator in your field (finance, marketing, or information technology) could help you stay abreast of new techniques and concepts that can help you to understand them and apply them to the performance of your job.

Another situation in which breadth of experience in a board member can be valuable is when your company or organization is undergoing a cultural change. Individuals with experience covering multiple corporate cultures can provide advice on how you can adjust to the new culture of your company. Breadth of experience in a board member can help you discover things of which you have limited knowledge.

As covered earlier, the challenges you face will influence the type of assistance you need (reinforcement, encouragement, ideas, perspective, et al.). You should seek candidates for your board whose strengths make them effective in providing the type of assistance you need. If you need reinforcement, seek individuals who are great at validating what others are attempting to accomplish. If you need encouragement, seek a board member who provides constructive criticism and who will check with you to ask you how you are progressing. If you need to clarify what you want or how to achieve it, seek someone who excels in generating ideas and options.

Style defines how individuals interact with others. It includes how they respond to requests, their approach to solving problems, and how they address challenges and issues. Style is a part of our personal *chemistry*, our input into the *mixture* that results when we interact with others. Individual styles include those who:

- Challenge
- Seek to collaborate
- Rely on logic
- Are emotional
- Are direct and formal
- Are indirect and informal

It is a human tendency to seek individuals whose style is close to our own. It makes us comfortable. However, interacting with people who are different may be more effective, as they will help us view things from a different perspective. This can uncover unseen obstacles that may be inhibiting your personal growth and development.

Striking an effective *chemical balance* with a board member can be challenging. How can you balance comfort versus the discomfort you may feel when you seek to discover? I suggest that you use the *sandpaper principle* for striking an effective balance:

> *Wood needs sanding to make a beautiful piece of furniture. The trick is to find the right type of sandpaper to prepare the wood. Too much friction will make the wood too thin. Too little friction will not make it smooth enough. Seek the balance that will provide enough, not too much or too little, friction.*

Consulting with someone who knows you well or perhaps a coach can help you apply the sandpaper principle to determining individuals you should approach to be members of your board.

Given the situation, you may work more effectively with members of your own or the opposite gender. Think about situations in the past in which you sought advice or assistance. In what types of situations did you interact most effectively with individuals of your own or the other gender? Based on the challenges you are facing and your experience, which gender would work best for you?

Ethnicity includes factors such as origin (US or foreign), race, and culture. Following are some situations that could lead you to considering ethnicity in determining whom you should approach to be a member of your board:

- Taking an assignment in a region in or outside the United States with which you are not familiar
- Establishing a relationship with a new boss who is from another part of the country or from outside the country
- Joining or assuming responsibility for managing a global team
- Seeking diversity in your thoughts
- Working in an environment in which you are a minority

Considering experience, strengths, style, gender, and ethnicity enables you to profile individuals you will approach to be members of your personal board of directors.

Summary: What, When, How

Structure

1. Sustain performance that meets or exceeds expectations.
2. Upgrade and refresh your product to keep pace with the needs of the employment marketplace.

Filing Cabinet

Situation/Need	Information on File

• Updating your career development plan
• Staying ahead of your competitors
• Identifying opportunities to increase your compensation
	• Research
	  o Visits to career websites
	  o Information provided by professional organizations
	  o Discussions with professional peers and your board members
	  o Curriculum of top-ranked colleges and universities
	  o Discussions with recent hires from other companies that are leaders in your discipline
	  o Discussions with recent graduates
	• Information gathered from attendance at vendor conferences
	• Discussions with search firm consultants
	• Information from job interviews
	• Discussions with individuals in transition
	• Discussions with personal board members

Sustaining your performance	• Setting the stage for establishing your annual performance objectives • Ensuring common understanding of performance expectations • Creating vision of the appraisal you want to receive • Personal Performance Monitoring System • Performance contingency planning
Identifying actions to improve how you are perceived by superiors, peers, and subordinates	• 360-degree survey feedback • Discussions with personal board members • Perspectives and observations from a coach
Re-launching your career	• Developing your product • Developing your personal brand • 6 P's of Marketing • Personal Selling Process

"When you're through changing, you're through."
—Bruce Barton, author and former head of BBDO Advertising Agency

126

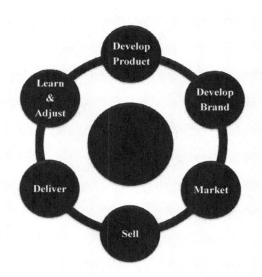

Conclusion

Global competition, pressure on profit margins, meeting quarterly expectations of the investment community, and changing business models will continue for several years. Companies will continue to respond to this environment, taking measures to do what their investors expect them to do—create value.

Unless you win the lottery or become a very savvy investor, you will need to rely on the management of your career to create value for yourself. Career management, just like business management, requires taking the right steps and applying the right information to the right situations. *The Business of Me* provides the structure for determining the right steps. These steps will guide you to the information you need. The information you gather and organize into your virtual filing cabinet will allow you to apply it to the right situations—the decisions you will make and the challenges you will address to maximize the personal value you create.

Reading *The Business of Me* will not answer all of your career management questions. However, it will provide a structure for determining what questions you need to ask and provide the criteria for evaluating the possible answers to those questions.

By using *The Business of Me*, you can optimize the use of your time, money, and other resources by leveraging the dependencies among the components of managing your career. *The Business of Me* can enable you to shift from being *managed by data* to *managing information* to maximize the return on your most important economic asset—your career.

Your Job ... Your Career ... Your Value

About the Author

Linwood Bailey is the founder and owner of Fields of Success, LLC. As a business and personal coach, Linwood partners with professionals to assist them in addressing the career management challenges presented by today's employment environment.

The foundation for Fields of Success is the been-there factor—Linwood has thirty-four years of experience managing functions and people in multiple industries and corporate cultures. His experience covers the pharmaceutical, consumer packaged, and durable goods industries. He has worked in the northeastern, midwestern, and southern regions of the United States. He has also managed global functions.

Linwood has experienced what today's professionals are experiencing, being the decision maker that impacted people as well as being impacted by decisions made by the companies for which he worked.

Linwood is a graduate of Coach University and earned his MBA at Indiana University and his undergraduate degree at Hampton University. He attained the rank of Captain in the US Army and is a Vietnam Veteran.

Linwood and his wife, JoAnn, reside in Granger, Indiana.

About Fields of Success

Fields of Success enables business professionals to get the most value from their most important economic asset—their careers. We help our clients create personal value by delivering coaching products and services to satisfy their specific needs. This includes:

- Positioning for exceptional pay raises, promotions, and career advancement
- Influencing individuals who make or influence talent management decisions
- Leveraging new capabilities, skills, and credentials such as an undergraduate or a graduate degree
- Understanding corporate cultures and politics
- Increasing personal effectiveness
- Improving job performance
- Improving relationships with managers, peers and subordinates
- Landing a new career opportunity after losing a position
- Making the transition from student to professional
- Returning to the workforce

Our clients benefit from the Fields of Success *been-there factor*—the thirty-four years of experience of its owner and founder, Linwood Bailey. Linwood managed people and finance, information technology, and business planning functions in multiple corporate cultures, industries, and regions. He has firsthand knowledge of the challenges that business professionals are encountering today, having been a decision maker that impacted individuals as well as being impacted by the decisions made by his employers.

Fields of Success provides the insight that its clients can use to develop and execute plans to satisfy their career management needs. This insight reflects an in-depth understanding of how companies operate, how effective relationships are established and managed, how talent is evaluated, how hiring and promotion decisions are made, and how opportunities are created for individual career advancement.

You can learn more about how Fields of Success can help you achieve your objectives by visiting the company's website, www.fieldsofsuccesscoaching. com. Fields of Success offers complimentary consultations that can help you determine the assistance you need.